PENGUIN E

MW00681252

Gluten Free

BIBLE

Gluten Free

BIBLE

Jacki Passmore

Contents

Introduction

Many people nowadays are sensitive to the protein gluten, with coeliac disease being an extreme case of gluten intolerance. Symptoms can include bloating, pain, diarrhoea or constipation and fatigue. Eating gluten can cause permanent damage to the small intestine by damaging the villi, the minuscule 'fingers' lining the small intestine, which absorb nutrients from food passing over them in the digestive process. By removing gluten from the diet, the digestive system can function in a normal, healthy way.

But unfortunately for the coeliac, gluten occurs in many everyday foods, and with frustrating frequency in processed and packaged foods.

Maintaining a diet free of gluten has become much easier than it was even a decade ago. More information is available, recipes created and adapted, and new products are flowing into supermarkets and health food stores.

Gluten-free basics

Following a gluten-free regime does require constant vigilance when shopping and dining out. And it calls for creativity in the kitchen so that eating gluten free doesn't have to be a hassle when it comes to sharing family meals and entertaining friends. The dishes in this book are designed to be enjoyed by everyone, gluten intolerant or not.

Grains containing gluten are wheat, barley, rye and oats, which means that most standard bread, cakes, biscuits and cereals are off limits. But gluten is also a common factor in the food processing industry, making unexpected appearances in all manner of foods from sweets to gravy powders, canned soups to ice-cream, and of course in the processing of beer and some other alcoholic beverages.

With so many products on the watch list, it makes sense to develop a repertoire of safe recipes, and keep the pantry stocked with gluten-free alternatives. Rice, including noodles, pasta sheets, flour, crumbs and cereals can play a major role. As can soy, although its taste is not to everyone's liking.

Corn ground into the fine meal we know as polenta has been a mainstream grain (think cornbread, tortillas, tacos and corn chips) in many parts of the world for thousands of years, while another old world grain coming back into vogue is the small grained quinoa which cooks crunchy and almost transparent.

Nutty tasting buckwheat has long been popular in Japan and northern European countries, and although it does contain a gluten analogue, many people with gluten allergy find they can tolerate it quite happily. These three grains are satisfying stand-ins for wheat based grain products and satisfactorily replace couscous, semolina and burghul (cracked wheat).

Potatoes, chickpeas and other legumes, arrowroot, tapioca and sago are high-starch food products which can be used variously for thickening, baking and in desserts.

To simplify matters you can now readily purchase gluten-free plain and self-raising flours which are a composite of rice, maize (corn) and tapioca, sometimes with soy flour or glutinous rice flour. There are gluten-free cake, biscuit, pastry, muffin and bread mixes, gravies, custards and also food additives which help to give gluten-free flour that elasticity that normally comes from gluten.

With a well stocked food cupboard and a positive approach, cooking for a gluten-free diet can become a pleasure rather than a grudging chore.

Coeliac, or wheat intolerant?

Not everyone experiencing difficulties with digesting wheat products may be suffering from coeliac disease. Wheat intolerance is an increasing medical problem, as are intolerances and allergies to a number of other major food products such as dairy foods, peanuts and certain seafood. Such intolerances and allergies may have an inherent factor, or may result from general decline in good health due to a multitude of factors including stress, overwork, viral illnesses and poor nutrition. Removing the offending element from the diet, while at the same time addressing other health and lifestyle issues, can see you on the road to recovery. But in the meantime, a diet free of wheat and perhaps all other gluten-bearing foods, makes sound medical and nutritional sense.

Healthy and happy eating gluten-free

Maintaining a gluten-free diet does not mean sacrificing taste and originality, nor does it require the elimination or moderation of any other ingredients except those containing gluten. So unless you choose otherwise, all your favourite puddings, soups and mains are still on the table, as are breads, pizzas, biscuits and cakes — with a gluten-free twist.

Breakfast & brunch

Gluten-free bread may not toast up as toothsome and crunchy as wheat bread, and most of the popular cereals are off limits, but breakfast need not be a nightmare for the gluten intolerant. Individualise a muesli blend using permissible cereals, dried fruit, nuts and seeds. Spend a few minutes at the stove making hotcakes or sweet corn cakes to serve with bacon, ham or smoked salmon. Invent your own American style breakfast by topping pancakes and maple syrup with crispy prosciutto. Replace toast with grilled cornbread or corn tortillas, and fry gluten-free bread into French toast with cinnamon sugar. Go Spanish with a potato and egg tortilla, or eggs served over grilled capsicum, and don't forget that old healthy, homely favourite, baked beans.

‹ Cinnamon French toast (page 8)

Cinnamon French toast

1 large egg

3 tablespoons milk or cream

3 tablespoons butter

2 thick slices gluten-free white,
   walnut or fruit bread

1–1½ tablespoons fine white sugar

1 teaspoon ground cinnamon

yoghurt or berries, to serve

Beat egg and milk or cream in a shallow bowl.

Heat a non-stick pan over medium-high heat using butter.

Soak bread in egg mixture for about 30 seconds, and then carefully lift onto the pan. Cook on one side until golden-brown and turn to cook the other side.

Sprinkle on sugar and cinnamon, and serve hot on its own or with yoghurt and berries.

 I've found this recipe is less successful with wholemeal gluten-free bread or bread containing soy flour.

SERVES 2

Scrambled eggs with cornbread, spinach & smoked salmon

60 g fresh or frozen leaf spinach

4—5 teaspoons butter

1—2 thick slices cornbread (page 239)

2 eggs, beaten with 1 tablespoon water

salt and freshly ground black pepper

1—2 slices smoked salmon

In a saucepan cover spinach with lightly salted boiling water and leave to wilt or thaw, and then drain very well. Add a teaspoon of butter and leave in the saucepan, covered, to keep warm.

Put the cornbread on a hot plate lightly sprayed with oil, to toast on both sides.

Season the beaten eggs and cook in a small pan with 2–3 teaspoons of butter, until the eggs are just beginning to set. Do not overcook.

Butter the toast, and place scrambled eggs on one piece. Add spinach and smoked salmon on the side, and season generously with black pepper. Serve at once.

SERVES 1

Big breakfast with homemade tomato sauce

2–3 gluten-free sausages

2 field mushrooms

1 large tomato, cut in half

2 teaspoons rice crumbs

1 teaspoon chopped parsley

salt and freshly ground black pepper

a pinch of dried thyme (optional)

4 eggs

1 tablespoon milk or cream (optional)

butter or oil, for frying

2–4 slices gluten-free bread, toasted and lightly buttered

TOMATO SAUCE

1 large onion, finely chopped

2–3 cloves garlic, chopped

1.5 kg ripe tomatoes, chopped

1½ teaspoons sugar

salt and freshly ground black pepper

dried or fresh thyme and/or oregano

chopped fresh basil and/or parsley (optional), extra for garnish

To make the tomato sauce, place onion, garlic, tomatoes and sugar in a saucepan and simmer for almost an hour, stirring frequently. Season with salt and pepper and blend to a purée in a food processor blender, or press through a fine sieve to make a smooth sauce. If adding herbs, return sauce to the heat for a few minutes before stirring them in. Cool. >

Heat the grill to medium-hot. Place sausages, mushrooms and tomato, cut side up, on a grill tray.

Sprinkle tomato with salt, pepper, parsley, thyme (if using) and rice crumbs. Lightly season mushrooms and brush with oil. Cook for about 8 minutes, turning sausages several times. When sausages are almost done, beat eggs with milk or cream (if using), adding salt and pepper.

Heat a small saucepan and add 1 tablespoon butter or a little oil. Pour in the egg and cook, stirring continually, on medium heat until the egg is barely set. Remove immediately from the heat.

Serve eggs with toast, tomato, mushrooms and sausages on the side. Garnish with fresh herbs, and serve at once with the tomato sauce.

SERVES 2

Eggs benedict

2 thick slices gluten-free bread

butter

1 teaspoon vinegar

4 fresh eggs

2 slices ham off the bone or 4 slices smoked
  salmon

2–3 tablespoons bottle hollandaise sauce

salt and freshly ground black pepper

Place the bread under a grill, in a toaster or in a hot ribbed pan to grill on both sides. Butter lightly and keep warm.

Bring a small deep saucepan of water to the boil and add the vinegar. Break an egg into a cup. When the water is bubbling, stir with the handle of a wooden spoon and slide the egg into the centre of the swirling water. The white will wrap around the yolk as the egg spins. Cook for about 3 minutes, then lift out, keeping warm. Cook remaining eggs in the same way.

Set toast on plates and top with ham or salmon. Place well drained poached eggs on top and smother with hollandaise sauce. Season and serve at once.

SERVES 2

Huevos rancheros (Spanish eggs with capsicum & grilled tortillas)

1 red capsicum, cut into
  narrow strips

1 green capsicum, cut into
  narrow strips

1 small salad onion, cut in
  half and finely sliced

2 tablespoons olive oil

salt and freshly ground
  black pepper

½ teaspoon dried thyme or
  1½ teaspoons chopped
  fresh thyme

1–2 tablespoons chopped flat leaf
  parsley or coriander

4 corn tortillas

4 tablespoons grated mild cheese

4 eggs

In a non-stick pan sauté capsicum and onion in olive oil over medium heat until very soft (about 8 minutes). Add thyme and parsley or coriander and season to taste.

Sprinkle grated cheese over tortillas and grill until lightly browned and the cheese is bubbling.

Heat a large non-stick pan and fry eggs sunny side up.

Place a tortilla on each plate, cover with capsicum and top with an egg. Serve at once.

SERVES 4

Spanish omelette (potato tortilla)

2 large floury potatoes, peeled and cubed

4 tablespoons olive oil

1 small onion, finely chopped

2 cloves garlic, chopped

1½ teaspoons chopped fresh rosemary
   or ½ teaspoon dried rosemary

salt and freshly ground black pepper

5 eggs

½ cup chopped fresh parsley or a mix
   of parsley and basil

Spread potatoes in a non-stick frying pan and add the oil. Cover and cook on medium heat for about 12 minutes, shaking the pan from time to time to turn the potatoes. Once potatoes are tender and lightly browned, remove to a plate.

Preheat the oven to 200°C or grill to very hot.

In the same pan sauté the onion and garlic to lightly brown, and return the potatoes, arranging them evenly. Sprinkle on rosemary, salt and pepper.

Beat the eggs with the chopped herbs and pour evenly over the potatoes.

On medium heat cook for about 7 minutes until the underside is lightly browned. Transfer to the oven or grill and cook until the top is brown and firm. Let rest for a few minutes, and then slide out onto a plate. Cut into wedges to serve.

SERVES 4–8

Hotcakes

1¼ cups gluten-free plain flour

¼ cup gluten substitute (gluten-free gluten)

1 teaspoon gluten-free baking powder

½ teaspoon salt

2 cups milk

2 egg whites, beaten to soft peaks

ghee or oil, for frying

Sift plain flour, gluten substitute, baking powder and salt into a bowl and add the milk to make a thick batter. Fold in the egg whites and let rest for 5 minutes.

Heat a non-stick pan and add 1 teaspoon oil or ghee. Add heaped tablespoons of the batter, 3–4 at a time, and cook for about 2½ minutes on each side, turning once, until golden-brown and puffy.

Serve warm, layered with leg ham and tomato chutney or smoked salmon and sour cream, or serve with whipped butter and maple syrup, or yoghurt and berries. >

These hotcakes have infinite variations.

Add 80 g grated tasty cheese and 2–3 tablespoons chopped fresh herbs.

Add 80 g grated tasty cheese and 80 g cooked, well drained spinach, and black pepper.

Add 80 g grated tasty cheese, 100 g drained corn and 2 tablespoons chopped coriander.

Add 140 g diced smoked salmon and 2 tablespoons chopped dill tips.

Add 1 grated green apple (excess juice squeezed out), and 1½ teaspoons ground cinnamon or 2 tablespoons finely chopped walnuts.

MAKES 8–10

Buckwheat & polenta pancakes with banana & maple syrup

½ cup fine polenta

½ cup buckwheat flour

½ cup gluten-free self-raising flour

1 large egg

1 cup milk

⅓ teaspoon salt

1½ teaspoons baking powder

butter or ghee, for frying

2–3 bananas, sliced

2–3 tablespoons maple or golden syrup or runny honey

In a bowl combine the polenta and flours and beat in the egg and milk, salt and baking powder to make a soft batter. Let it sit for 10 minutes.

Heat 2–3 teaspoons butter or ghee in a non-stick pan and fry large spoonfuls of the batter until golden-brown on both sides, and lightly puffed.

Serve pancakes with bananas and honey, maple or golden syrup.

SERVES 2–3

Egg & bacon pies   *Nov. 23 — 3 stars*

4 slices gluten-free bread
butter
4 slices bacon, rind removed
4 eggs
1 tomato, sliced
salt and freshly ground black pepper
chopped chives and/or parsley

Use a round biscuit cutter to cut out pieces of bread to fit the bottom of small round pie tins or large muffin tins. Butter bread on both sides and press into the tins.

Preheat the oven to 230°C. Lightly fry the bacon in a non-stick pan for about 1 minute, turning once. (Make sure bacon remains soft.)

Lay the bacon around the sides of the tin, overlapping the ends. Break an egg into each tin and cover with a slice of tomato. Season and place in the oven for about 15 minutes, or until the bacon is crisp and the egg firm.

Carefully remove pies to warmed plates, garnish with chives or parsley and serve.

SERVES 4

Muesli

8 cups mixed gluten-free cereal
½ cup sultanas
½ cup banana chips
1 cup fruit and nut medley
milk and/or yoghurt, to serve

Combine the cereal, fruit and nuts and mix well.

Store in an airtight container for 1½–2 months.

Serve with milk and/or yoghurt.

Sweet corn cakes

2 corn cobs (250 g frozen corn)

3 thick slices (about 120 g) gluten-free bread

1 teaspoon gluten-free baking powder

3 tablespoons chopped parsley or coriander

1 teaspoon ground cumin

¾ teaspoon salt

⅓ cup gluten-free self-raising flour

2 large eggs, separated

olive oil, for frying

With a sharp knife cut corn from the cobs and boil in lightly salted water for 2–3 minutes. Drain and set aside to cool.

Cut bread into cubes, place in a food processor and process into crumbs. Add baking powder, herbs, cumin, salt, flour, egg yolks and a third of the corn and process until well mixed. Beat the egg whites until slightly frothy, but not peaky, and fold into the flour and crumb mixture, together with the remaining corn.

Heat 3–4 tablespoons olive oil and fry the batter into 4–6 cakes, for about 3 minutes on each side, until golden-brown and cooked. Serve hot or cold.

 Serve with grilled bacon or oven-roasted tomatoes and eggs for breakfast, and for brunch add a small-leaf salad.

SERVES 3–4

Homemade baked beans

2 cups dried white cannellini beans

½ cup dark brown sugar

½ cup cider vinegar

3 tablespoons dark soy sauce

1 large onion, finely chopped

2 teaspoons mustard powder

3 tablespoons tomato paste

Soak beans in a saucepan overnight in cold water, changing the water once. Drain and return to the saucepan and add 1½ litres of cold water. Run your fingers through the beans, rubbing them lightly to encourage the skins to loosen and float to the surface. Skim off and discard.

Simmer the beans on medium heat for about 45 minutes, skimming occasionally. Drain the beans, reserving the cooking liquid.

Preheat the oven to 140°C. (300° F — close to 350° F)

Combine the remaining ingredients in a large casserole dish and add the drained beans and about 1 cup of the reserved cooking liquid.

Cover with a lid or a double thickness of aluminium foil and bake for at least 2 hours, stirring occasionally, and adding more of the cooking liquid if the liquid in the casserole begins to dry up. >

Tender, creamy homemade baked beans are a favourite breakfast and snack food. Unfortunately, canned beans can sometimes contain gluten. If you love beans, you'll want to try these, and as they take time to cook, it makes sense to do enough for two or more meals. Note that salt is not added, as salt in cooking water makes beans tough.

SERVES 8

Breakfast muffins

1 slice bacon, finely diced

1 spring onion, finely chopped

70 g corn kernels or finely diced capsicum

80 g butter

2 eggs

1 teaspoon gluten-free baking powder

½ teaspoon salt

⅔ cup milk

1½ cups gluten-free self-raising flour

Preheat oven to 200°C.

Sauté the bacon, spring onion and corn or capsicum in all of the butter in a non-stick pan over medium-low heat for 3–4 minutes. Remove from heat and set aside to partially cool.

In a mixing bowl beat the eggs with baking powder, salt and milk and add to the flour. When half mixed in, add the contents of the sauté pan, including all of the butter and mix well.

Spoon into six non-stick muffin pans and bake for about 15 minutes, until golden. Test with a skewer in the centre of a muffin. It should come out dry. Serve hot or at room temperature.

MAKES 6 LARGE MUFFINS

Snacks & starters

Finger foods and nibbles, served tapas style with drinks, zing with flavour and creativity when they go gluten free. Why hanker for party pies and toast canapés when there are crisp tortilla chips with dips, crunchy prawn crackers or spicy lamb samosas with coriander chutney? When there's garlicky chorizo to grill with potato, haloumi cheese to skewer with salami and capsicum, and olives to stuff and coat with cheesy crumbs. Mediterranean flavours, Asian seasonings, and ever-popular classics like crumbed camembert make for deliciously easy snacks or entrées.

< Prawn crackers with tuna tartare
(page 32)

Prawn crackers with tuna tartare

24 dried prawn crackers

1½ cups oil

250 g fresh tuna of sashimi quality, finely chopped

1½ tablespoons finely chopped spring onion

1½ tablespoons finely chopped fresh coriander

1½–2 teaspoons finely chopped fresh basil or dill

3–4 teaspoons lime juice

3 teaspoons fish sauce (or salt and freshly ground
   black pepper)

extra fresh coriander leaves, or small dill sprigs

Heat the oil and fry prawn crackers until they puff and turn crisp (about
20 seconds). Lift out and drain on paper towels. Leave to cool.

Combine the chopped tuna, spring onion, herbs, lime juice and fish sauce
or seasoning in a bowl.

Arrange crackers on a serving platter and top each with a spoonful of the
tartare. Decorate with coriander or dill, and serve at once.

Add finely chopped sun-dried tomato or marinated char-grilled capsicum to topping. Make it into a vegetarian topping using finely chopped marinated eggplant, mushrooms, artichokes, semi-dried tomato and capsicum instead of the tuna.

MAKES 24

Tortilla crisps with cheesy bean dip

3 corn tortillas

1½ cups olive or vegetable oil

½ can red kidney beans or three bean mix,
   drained

2 tablespoons salsa

2 tablespoons grated fetta cheese

2–3 tablespoons sour cream

2 teaspoons chopped chives or coriander

Cut each tortilla into twelve little triangles.

Heat oil to medium-high and fry tortilla chips about eight at a time, until crisp. Drain over paper towels, and let cool.

Press the beans through a sieve, discarding skins. Beat in salsa, cheese and sour cream. Stir in herbs.

Pile dip into a bowl, place in the centre of a serving platter and surround with tortilla crisps.

MAKES 36

Char-grilled skewers of haloumi, salami & capsicum

250 g gluten-free salami

180 g haloumi cheese

180 g char-grilled or marinated capsicum, drained

olive oil spray

12 long toothpicks or short satay skewers

Remove the skin from salami and cut into twenty-four chunks. Cut haloumi into twelve pieces and capsicum into twenty-four strips.

Onto each skewer thread in this order: a piece of salami, a folded strip of capsicum, a cube of cheese, another folded strip of capsicum, and finish with another piece of salami.

Spray with olive oil and grill lightly until cheese softens.

 A one-stop shop at the deli counter of your local supermarket will provide all the requirements for these appealing skewers. Check before you buy to ensure salami is gluten free.

MAKES 12

Grilled chorizo & paprika potatoes

2 gluten-free chorizo sausages

5—6 new potatoes

salt

olive oil, for frying

½ teaspoon smoked or sweet paprika

½ teaspoon dried thyme

15–20 toothpicks

Cut chorizo into 1-cm slices and set aside.

Cut unpeeled potatoes into 1-cm slices and place in a steamer. Sprinkle lightly with salt and steam for about 8 minutes, until almost cooked.

Oil a barbecue hotplate or non-stick pan and cook the sliced potatoes and chorizo for about 1 minute on each side, until browned. Sprinkle with salt, paprika and thyme and pierce in twos and threes on toothpicks. Serve warm.

MAKES ABOUT 15–20

Cold rice-paper rolls

½ punnet fresh enoki mushrooms or 3 sliced button mushrooms

12 small lettuce leaves

1 medium carrot, in matchstick strips

⅔ celery stick, in matchstick strips

2 spring onions, in matchstick strips

100 g fresh bean sprouts, blanched and refreshed (or ½ punnet snow pea sprouts)

12–15 cooked, peeled prawns, or 150 g shredded cooked chicken or firm tofu

basil or coriander leaves

12–15 Vietnamese rice paper wraps (banh trang)

sweet chilli sauce

Vietnamese dipping sauce, to serve

Prepare the fillings and arrange in groups on a tray.

Fill a bowl with very hot water and place a clean tea towel beside it.

To make the rolls, dip rice papers into hot water one at a time until softened, spread on the towel and place some of each of the filling ingredients in the middle of the wrap. Add ½ teaspoon of sweet chilli.

Fold bottom of wrap over, fold top over, and roll up. Serve with Vietnamese dipping sauce.

MAKES 12–15

Coconut prawns

18 medium-large prawn cutlets

1 teaspoon crushed ginger

2 teaspoons fish sauce

½ teaspoon salt

3 tablespoons gluten-free corn flour

1½ cups shredded coconut

2 large egg whites

2–3 cups oil, for deep frying

sweet chilli or Vietnamese dipping sauce, to serve

Place cleaned prawns with tails intact in a bowl and add ginger, fish sauce and salt, stir to evenly coat, and let sit for 10 minutes.

Spread flour and coconut in separate shallow bowls. Beat egg whites until fluffy, but not peaky, in another bowl. One by one coat the prawns lightly with cornflour, then dip in egg and coat with coconut.

Heat the oil for deep frying and test with a cube of bread. It should be medium-hot, requiring a few minutes for the bread to turn golden. Reduce heat slightly.

Fry the prawns in two batches, until the coconut is golden-brown and the prawn meat white and firm (about 2½ minutes). Remove with a wire scoop and drain on a rack over paper towels. Serve hot with sweet chilli or Vietnamese dipping sauce.

MAKES 18

Cheese-crumbed stuffed olives

12 large green olives, pitted and stuffed
   with fetta cheese or anchovies

2 slices gluten-free sour dough bread

⅓ cup grated parmesan cheese

1 large egg

2–3 tablespoons rice flour

1 cup olive oil

Dry the olives on paper towels. Trim crust from bread, cut into cubes and place in a food processor. Grind to crumbs, and add the parmesan. Spread on a plate.

Beat egg in a shallow bowl and spread rice flour on a plate. Roll olives in flour, dip into egg and coat with the crumbs. If necessary, repeat the egg and crumbs.

Place olives on a plate and refrigerate for 15 minutes.

Heat the oil in a frying pan to medium-hot and gently fry the olives until golden-brown. Remove with a slotted spoon and drain briefly on a rack over a double thickness of paper towel, then serve.

MAKES 12

Polenta crisps with marinated capsicum & yoghurt cheese

½ recipe soft polenta (page 170)

oil, for deep-frying

4 slices marinated char-grilled capsicum,
    eggplant or artichokes

120 g yoghurt cheese (or cream cheese)

24 stuffed green olives, to serve

Cut polenta into twenty-four 3-cm × 3-cm squares about 1-cm thick.

Heat oil in a wok or large frying pan and fry polenta squares until golden-brown. Lift out and drain on paper towels.

Drain capsicum, eggplant or artichokes well and cut into strips.

Spread cheese on each polenta square, top with a folded strip of capsicum, eggplant or artichokes and pierce with a stuffed olive on a toothpick.

MAKES 24

Spicy lamb samosas

4 large spring roll sheets

1½ tablespoons butter or oil

250 g lean minced lamb (or beef)

½ teaspoon crushed ginger

1 small onion, very finely chopped

½ teaspoon ground turmeric

½ teaspoon ground cumin

½ teaspoon ground chilli

salt and freshly ground black pepper

2–3 tablespoons peas

1–2 tablespoons gluten-free breadcrumbs

2 tablespoons chopped fresh coriander or mint

2–3 cups oil

Place spring roll sheets between clean tea towels to thaw.

Heat the butter or oil in a frying pan or wok and sauté minced meat, onion and ginger until meat is lightly browned.

Add spices and seasoning and cook for 1 minute, stirring. Add peas and ⅓ cup water and simmer, stirring occasionally, for 5–6 minutes until peas are tender and the liquid absorbed. Stir in breadcrumbs and herbs.

Working one sheet of pastry at a time cut into four even sized strips and fold bottom end of strip over to form a triangle.

Add 2–3 teaspoons of filling and fold up the pastry to form triangular shaped samosa, moistening the end flap to stick it down.

Heat oil in a frying pan to medium-high and fry samosas to golden-brown. Serve warm or cold.

MAKES 24

Crumbed camembert with cranberry jelly

1 × 125-g wheel camembert cheese

2 tablespoons cashew nuts

¾ cup gluten-free fresh breadcrumbs

⅓ cup cornflour

1 large egg, beaten with 1 tablespoon milk

light olive oil, for frying

2–3 tablespoons cranberry jelly

2–3 teaspoons dried craisins, chopped (optional)

fresh herbs or small-leaf salad, to serve

Cut the camembert into 4–6 wedges.

Crush cashews in a food processor and mix with breadcrumbs. Spread cornflour on a plate, egg in a shallow bowl and crumb mix in another. Coat cheese wedges with flour, then egg and lastly crumbs. Repeat egg and crumbs if needed, to coat evenly. Set on a plate and refrigerate for 20 minutes.

Heat olive oil in a shallow pan and gently fry crumbed cheese until golden, turning to brown each surface. Serve with cranberry jelly, dried craisins (if using) and garnish with fresh herbs or small-leaf lettuce.

SERVES 2–3

Onion bhajias

2 medium onions (or use 1 onion and 2 cups small-leaf spinach)

¾ cup besan (chickpea flour)

3 tablespoons gluten-free self-raising flour

1 teaspoon gluten-free baking powder

2 teaspoons ground coriander

1 teaspoon cumin seeds

½ teaspoon ground chilli

salt

1 large egg, beaten

2—3 tablespoons chopped fresh coriander (optional)

oil, for deep-frying

sweet chilli sauce or fruit chutney, to serve

small salad leaves, to serve

Peel the onions and cut in half. Slice thinly and blanch in boiling water. Drain well and set aside.

Sift flours and baking powder into a bowl and add the spices, salt and beaten egg. Mix well, adding enough water to make a thick batter, about ½ cup. Stir in herbs, spinach (if using) and onion.

Heat about 5 cm of oil in a wok or large pan. Carefully slice tablespoons of the batter into the oil to fry until golden-brown and floating to the surface, about 2—3 minutes depending on their size. Drain well and serve hot with sweet chilli sauce or fruity chutney and small salad leaves.

MAKES 16—24 (SERVES 4—6)

Sesame chicken strips with plum sauce

250 g chicken breast, skinned and boned

salt and freshly ground black pepper

1 teaspoon crushed ginger

2 tablespoons cornflour or arrowroot

1–2 eggs, beaten

¾–1 cup sesame seeds

2–3 cups oil

spicy plum sauce or sweet chilli sauce, to serve

small-leaf lettuce mix, to serve

Cut chicken into strips, season with salt, pepper and ginger and knead lightly with fingers to press in seasonings. Coat lightly with cornflour or arrowroot, shaking off excess. Dip into egg, and coat with sesame seeds.

Heat the oil in a wok or frying pan to reasonably high. Add half the chicken strips, lower heat a little, and fry for 2½–3 minutes, turning once or twice. Remove to a plate covered with paper towel to drain. Fry the remaining chicken in the same way.

Scatter lettuce leaves over four plates and arrange chicken strips over. Serve each with a small plate of dipping sauce.

SERVES 4

Croque monsieur (grilled cheese toast)

2 thick slices gluten-free bread

2 teaspoons Dijon mustard

2 thin slices ham

1–2 tablespoons grated tasty cheese (optional)

CHEESE SAUCE

50 g butter

⅓ cup gluten-free plain flour

2 cups milk

salt and freshly ground black pepper

⅓ teaspoon grated nutmeg (optional)

1 cup grated tasty cheese

To make the cheese sauce, melt butter in a small saucepan and mix in flour. Stir with a wire whisk, until it thickens, then add ¾ cup milk and whisk over medium heat. When smooth add the remaining milk, salt and pepper and whisk gently until the sauce thickens and becomes smooth. Add nutmeg (if using). Stir in cheese. (If the sauce thins out after a few minutes, return to medium heat and stir gently until it thickens.)

Toast the bread and set on a grill tray. Spread toast with mustard, add a slice of ham, and top with cheese sauce. Add grated cheese (if using). Place under a hot grill to cook until cheese bubbles. Serve at once.

— add sliced tomato / top fresh basil

 Vary the cheese sauce by substituting the tasty cheese for ½ cup grated parmesan, ½ cup crumbled blue cheese, or ¾ cup soft fetta.

SERVES 2

Vegetable pakoras

110 g besan (chickpea flour)

60 g gluten-free self-raising flour

1 teaspoon gluten-free baking powder

⅓ teaspoon ground turmeric

½ teaspoon ground chilli

1 teaspoon mild curry powder or garam masala

1½ teaspoons salt

oil, for deep-frying

500 g mixed diced vegetables

Sift the flours, baking powder, spices and salt into a bowl and add enough water (approximately 1 cup) to make a smooth, creamy batter. Set aside for 10 minutes.

Heat oil for deep frying in a wok or large pan, to medium-hot and test with a cube of bread. It should turn golden-brown within about 40 seconds.

Stir vegetables into the batter, mixing well. Slide heaped tablespoons of the mixture into the oil to cook until golden-brown and floating (about 2 minutes). Drain on a rack over paper towels, before serving.

Besan (chickpea flour) gives an appealing nutty flavour to these vegetable cakes which can be served as a main course, appetiser or snack, with a spicy chutney or sweet chilli sauce. If using frozen diced vegetables thaw in a colander so they drain thoroughly.

SERVES 4–6

Potato, cheese & bacon puffs

400 g potatoes, peeled and cubed

50 g butter

1 small clove garlic, crushed

2–3 slices pancetta or bacon, finely chopped

2 spring onions, finely chopped

½ cup finely grated tasty cheese

1 egg, separated

1 teaspoon gluten-free baking powder

1 tablespoon potato starch, cornflour or arrowroot

2–3 cups oil

Boil the potatoes in lightly salted water until tender. Drain well and mash over gentle heat to dry them out, adding garlic and half the butter.

Fry pancetta or bacon with onions in remaining butter until crisp. Stir into potatoes, with the cheese and egg yolk.

Whisk egg white with baking powder, stir into potatoes, adding the starch. Mix well.

With damp hands form into small balls and deep fry in hot oil until golden. Serve hot.

MAKES 24

Lunch

Experiment with pine nuts and breadcrumbs fried in olive oil as a crunchy topping for delicious vegetables, and sesame seeds as a coating for fish and chicken. Slice and dice vegetables into a frittata and marry rich and flavoursome smoked salmon with simple potato cakes. With gluten-free bread options, sandwiches, pizzas, burgers and wraps are back in the lunchbox. Or try something different, like tostadas of crisp-fried corn tortillas smothered in creamy crab meat. Great tastes every time.

< Felafel with cucumber mint
yoghurt (page 56)

Felafel with cucumber mint yoghurt

200 g gluten-free felafel mix

2 cups oil

¾ cup natural yoghurt

2 tablespoons grated cucumber, well drained

2–3 teaspoons finely chopped mint

a pinch each of salt and ground cumin

Mix felafel mixture with water according to directions on pack, and set aside to soften. With damp hands form into small balls.

Heat oil in a wok or frying pan and fry the felafel to golden-brown for 2½–3 minutes, over medium heat. Drain on paper towels.

Whisk yoghurt with cucumber, mint and spices and transfer to a dish, for dipping. Place in the centre of a platter and surround with the felafel. Serve hot.

MAKES ABOUT 24

Tartlets of smoked salmon & goat's cheese

1 recipe gluten-free shortcrust
   pastry (page 249)

120 g smoked salmon, diced

100 g soft goat's cheese

90 g mascarpone or sour cream

12 capers or small dill sprigs

Preheat oven to 180°C. Grease 12 small tart tins.

Roll out pastry, cut into rounds to fit the tart tins and press into tins. Prick with a fork and bake for about 12 minutes, until lightly golden-brown.

Mix goat's cheese, mascarpone or cream and salmon and spoon into tart shells.

Return tarts to the oven just long enough to warm through.

Garnish with a caper or dill sprig, and serve.

MAKES 12

Bruschetta with char-grilled capsicum & soft fetta

120 g marinated char-grilled capsicum,
   cut into strips
4 slices gluten-free bread
1½ tablespoons olive tapenade
100 g soft fetta cheese
handful rocket leaves

Brush the bread lightly with some of the oil drained from the capsicum and place on a hot ribbed grill to toast.

When bread is toasted on both sides, spread one side with tapenade followed by soft fetta. Add a few rocket leaves and cover with strips of capsicum.

Serve at once.

MAKES 4

Chilled tomatoes with white bean & herb stuffing

4 hydroponic tomatoes

½ can white beans, well drained

1 small red salad onion, very finely
  chopped

2 tablespoons chopped herbs (basil,
  dill or oregano, and flat leaf parsley)

grated zest and juice of ½ orange

salt and freshly ground black pepper

Slice the tops off the tomatoes and use a teaspoon or melon scoop to remove the fleshy core and seeds. Turn upside down onto paper towel and leave for 10 minutes to drain.

In a bowl combine the beans, onion, herbs and orange. Season to taste and mix well.

Very finely chop the sliced-off tops of the tomatoes and stir into the mixture.

Fill the tomatoes with the bean stuffing, and serve chilled.

SERVES 4

Tuna crusted with black sesame seeds

350 g fresh tuna

salt and freshly ground black pepper

3 tablespoons black sesame seeds (or a mix of black and white)

2 tablespoons light olive oil or sesame oil

2 small cucumbers, thinly shaved

1 cup mizuna leaves or ½ punnet snow pea sprouts, trimmed

2–3 tablespoons finely shredded spring-onion greens

1½ tablespoons gluten-free teriyaki seasoning

Cut the tuna into four even sized pieces and season lightly. Coat with the sesame seeds, pressing them on.

Heat a non-stick pan and moisten with the oil.

Cook tuna on both sides until firm and crisp, with the inside remaining pink and rare, about 3 minutes in all. Set aside to cool.

In a salad bowl combine cucumber, mizuna or sprouts and spring-onion greens and toss with teriyaki seasoning (or a gluten-free Asian salad dressing).

Place a small mound of salad on each plate and top with tuna. Serve at once.

SERVES 4

Make-in-minutes salmon mousse

1 × 415-g can red salmon

1 tablespoon very finely chopped
   red onion

2 teaspoons finely chopped
   capers

½ cup mascarpone or sour
   cream

lemon juice

freshly ground black pepper

SALAD

2—3 oranges, segmented

1—2 bunches watercress, broken
   into small sprigs

vinaigrette or Italian dressing

Drain the salmon well and scrape off any grey skin. Place in a food processor with the onion, capers and mascarpone or cream and process well. Add lemon juice and pepper to taste.

To make the salad, combine the orange segments and watercress. Toss the salad with vinaigrette or Italian dressing.

Serve mousse in small pots or mound casually on plates, with the orange and watercress salad at the side.

SERVES 4—6

Grilled eggplant with sour cream & chilli jam

1 large globe eggplant
salt
olive oil, for frying
baby spinach leaves, lightly dressed
¾ cup sour cream
2 tablespoons chilli jam or spicy chutney

Thickly slice the unpeeled eggplant to make eight slices. Sprinkle generously with salt and let sit for 10–15 minutes. Rinse under running cold water, drain and dry with paper towels. Brush or spray with olive oil and cook on a hot plate or non-stick pan, turning several times, until softened and golden-brown, but still holding their shape.

Stack two slices, interleaving with baby spinach leaves.

Top each eggplant stack with sour cream and chilli jam or chutney, and serve.

MAKES 4

Tikka fish skewers with yoghurt & pappadams

200 g firm thick fish fillets (such as rockling or swordfish), cut into bite-sized cubes

6 tablespoons natural yoghurt

3 teaspoons tandoori marinade

½ teaspoon cracked black pepper

olive oil spray

4 pappadams, plain or spiced

1 large lettuce leaf, finely shredded

2–3 teaspoons chopped fresh mint

spicy chutney, to serve

Place fish in a bowl with 2 tablespoons of the yoghurt, the tandoori marinade, pepper and mix well. Leave for 10 minutes, then thread onto four skewers.

Spray skewers with oil and grill, turning several times, until fish is cooked (about 4–5 minutes). Microwave pappadams two or three at a time, for about 15 seconds each, until puffed and dry.

Place some lettuce in the centre of a plate, add 1–2 skewers, a spoonful of the remaining yoghurt scattered with chopped mint, and 1–2 pappadams on the side. Serve at once, with spicy chutney.

 If preferred, remove fish from skewers before serving.

SERVES 2–4

Chicken, asparagus & cheese wrapped in prosciutto

2 small chicken breasts

4 thick asparagus spears,
   parboiled in lightly salted water

6 tablespoons grated cheese

8 slices prosciutto

olive oil, for frying

baby salad leaves, to serve

Cut chicken breasts in half and bat out until very thin. Season very sparingly with salt and pepper. Place a piece of asparagus on each, and add 1½ tablespoons grated cheese, roll up and squeeze into a log shape. Wrap with two pieces of prosciutto.

Fry the chicken on medium heat in a little olive oil until prosciutto is crisp (about 2 minutes), turning often. Microwave for about 1 minute to complete cooking and to melt the cheese.

Serve at once with baby salad leaves.

SERVES 2

Potato cakes with smoked salmon

450 g potatoes, peeled and cubed

salt and freshly ground black
  pepper

1½ tablespoons butter

2 tablespoons chopped fresh
  coriander, chives or parsley

3 tablespoons rice crumbs, fine
  polenta, besan (chickpea
  flour), rice flour or gluten-
  free plain flour

½ cup light olive oil, for shallow
  frying

8–12 slices smoked salmon

handful rocket or small-leaf
  lettuce leaves

Boil potatoes in salted water until tender. Drain well. Tip into a bowl and
mash smoothly, adding salt, pepper and butter, and the chopped herbs.
Shape into four or six patties and coat with the preferred crumbs or flour.

Heat a non-stick pan and add the oil. When reasonably hot, put in the
potato cakes to cook for about 1½ minutes on each side, until golden-
brown, turning carefully. Serve with salmon and greens.

You could serve these potato cakes with prosciutto or crisp bacon,
or for a more substantial meal with roast chicken or grilled fish.

SERVES 4–6

Baked stuffed capsicums

½ cup cracked buckwheat or quinoa

4 red capsicums or 2 medium-sized globe eggplants

3 tablespoons olive oil

1 small onion, finely chopped

1 clove garlic, crushed

200 g lean minced beef or lamb, or 1 gluten-free chorizo sausage

½ cup tomato and herb pasta sauce

2–3 tablespoons chopped flat-leaf parsley or a mix of parsley and basil

salt and freshly ground black pepper

¾ teaspoon sweet paprika

½ cup gluten-free breadcrumbs

Soak the buckwheat in boiling water for about 45 minutes and drain. (Soak quinoa for 20 minutes.)

Preheat the oven to 200°C.

Cut the tops from the capsicum and remove the seed cores, or cut the eggplant lengthwise in half and scoop out three quarters of the flesh, chopping it finely.

In a small non-stick pan heat half the oil and sauté the onion, garlic and minced meat for about 5 minutes, stirring frequently, until lightly browned. If using chorizo sausage, chop it finely, brown onions and then add chorizo and sauté briefly.

For eggplant stuffing, add the diced eggplant flesh.

Add pasta sauce and 3–4 tablespoons water and reduce heat. Simmer until most of the liquid has evaporated, and then add the drained buckwheat or quinoa, the herbs, salt and pepper to taste, and the paprika.

Stand the capsicum or eggplant side by side in a baking dish generously brushed with olive oil. Stuff with the prepared filling and smooth the tops.

Cover with breadcrumbs and drizzle with remaining oil.

Bake for about 25 minutes. Serve hot or cold.

 You could also use this filling for large zucchinis.

SERVES 4

Zucchini quiche

1 recipe shortcrust pastry (page 249)

2 zucchinis (about 350 g)

2 spring onions, finely chopped

4 eggs

1 cup cream

½ teaspoon dried oregano

salt and freshly ground black pepper

side vegetables or salad, to serve

Preheat the oven to 180°C.

Press or roll the pastry into a 23-cm quiche dish or cake tin, prick the base with a fork and place in the oven for 10 minutes.

Grate zucchini and spread zucchini and spring onions into the quiche base. Whisk eggs until creamy and stir in cream, oregano, salt and pepper and pour evenly over the zucchini. Bake for 35–40 minutes until the filling is firm and lightly golden.

Serve hot or at room temperature, with vegetables or a side salad.

SERVES 6–8

NN. 30 - 4. stars

Open burgers

1 large red salad onion, sliced

3 tablespoons olive oil

salt and freshly ground black
  pepper

5 thick slices gluten-free bread

1 small onion, roughly chopped

2 sprigs parsley

400 g minced beef

½ teaspoon dried thyme

1½ teaspoons grain mustard

3 tablespoons barbecue sauce

1 egg yolk

2 tablespoons cornflour or
  potato starch

1 large tomato, sliced

4 lettuce leaves or a handful
  of baby salad leaves

In a small pan gently fry the sliced onion in 1½ tablespoons olive oil until
very tender (about 8 minutes) stirring frequently. Season with salt and
pepper.

Set aside four slices of bread, and break the remaining slice into pieces.
Place bread pieces in a food processor and grind to crumbs. Add the
roughly chopped onion and the parsley and chop finely. Add minced beef,
thyme, mustard, 1 tablespoon barbecue sauce and the egg yolk and use
pulse control to mince together. (It may be necessary to divide the mixture
into two parts to prevent overloading the processor.)

Form into four patties and coat lightly with cornflour or potato starch. ❯

Heat a non-stick pan or grill and brush with remaining oil. Cook burger patties for about 3½ minutes on each side, until cooked through and well browned.

Lightly toast the bread and top each slice with lettuce, tomato, a cooked patty, a swirl of barbecue sauce and a mound of fried onions. Serve at once.

MAKES 4

Tuna & salad wrap

2 gluten-free wraps

1–2 small tins plain or seasoned tuna, drained

2–3 tablespoons mayonnaise

1 large tomato, sliced

2 large lettuce leaves, finely shredded

1 medium carrot, peeled and grated

snow pea or other sprouts (optional)

2–3 slices red salad onion, separated into rings

Wraps need to be warmed to make them pliable enough to roll. To warm in a microwave oven, wrap loosely in plastic wrap and heat for 20 seconds each. To warm in the oven enclose in foil and heat at 180°C for 5–6 minutes.

Mix tuna with mayonnaise. Along the centre of each wrap build up the filling first with lettuce, then tomato, sprouts (if using), carrot, onion and tuna. Roll, wrap and serve. >

Some popular mountain bread varieties are gluten-free – check the label. Alternatively, you can use the flatbread and wraps recipe on page 241, or corn tortillas.

For a variation, use finely chopped cooked chicken mixed with mayonnaise, sour cream or guacamole, instead of tuna.

MAKES 2

Tostadas with creamy crab meat

2–4 corn tortillas

4 tablespoons olive oil

1 small onion, finely chopped

1 cup (160 g) cooked or fresh
crab meat

3 teaspoons gluten-free
cornflour or arrowroot

1 cup milk or light cream

½ teaspoon crushed or fresh
chopped hot red chilli

salt and freshly ground black
pepper

4 tablespoons grated tasty cheese

guacamole, mild salsa and sour
cream (optional), to serve

Fry the tortillas in 3 tablespoons of the oil, turning once or twice, until golden and crisp, and set aside to drain.

Heat the remaining oil in a small saucepan and lightly brown the onion. Add crabmeat and warm through gently.

Mix cornflour or arrowroot, milk, chilli, salt and pepper and pour over the crab. Simmer, stirring frequently, until it thickens (about 3 minutes). Stir in half the cheese.

Heat the grill to hot. Place tortillas on an oven tray. Cover with the crab sauce and sprinkle on remaining cheese. Grill until cheese melts. Serve hot on their own, or with guacamole, salsa and sour cream.

SERVES 2

Potato & rosemary pizza slice

1 recipe thin-crust pizza base (page 247)

2 tablespoons extra-virgin olive oil

1 medium—large potato

2 cloves garlic, finely chopped

2—3 rosemary sprigs

flake salt

Preheat oven to 250°C.

With oiled fingers press pizza dough out into a thin rectangle on a biscuit tray, prick with a fork and set aside for a few minutes.

Use a vegetable peeler or mandolin to cut potato into thin slices, place in a bowl and pour on boiling water. Let sit for 4—5 minutes and then drain well and dry in a kitchen cloth.

Brush pizza dough with oil and prebake without topping for about 12 minutes.

Brush again with oil, spread potato slices on evenly and then scatter with the garlic, rosemary broken into points, and the salt.

Bake for about 12 minutes until lightly browned and crisp.
Cut into squares to serve.

— Last 3 mins, top with sliced tomatoes
— serve with fresh chopped basil / oregano

SERVES 2—4

Moroccan spiced chicken & cherry tomato pizza

1 recipe thin-crust pizza base (page 247)
150 g chicken breast, thinly sliced
2 teaspoons Moroccan chermoula seasoning
2 tablespoons olive oil
8 small cherry tomatoes, cut in half
60–80 g soft yoghurt cheese or Danish fetta
flake salt

Preheat oven to 250°C.

Cut pizza dough in half and with oiled fingers press out on two small pizza trays. Prick with a fork and set aside for a few minutes.

Toss chicken with chermoula seasoning, mixing well. Brush pizza bases with olive oil and bake without topping for about 12 minutes.

Arrange chicken evenly over each base. Scatter on tomatoes and little spoonfuls of cheese. Drizzle on any remaining oil and season with flake salt.

Bake for 12–15 minutes until crisp and golden. Serve at once.

SERVES 2

Fried whiting fillets on toast with capsicum relish

8 fresh whiting fillets

salt and freshly ground black pepper

¼ cup gluten-free cornflour

2 tablespoons light olive oil

1½ tablespoons butter

2 slices gluten-free bread, toasted and lightly buttered

CAPSICUM RELISH

1 large red capsicum, diced

1 medium red salad onion, diced

1 clove garlic, crushed

2 tablespoons olive oil

2 tablespoons soft brown sugar

2 tablespoons balsamic vinegar

Prepare the capsicum relish in advance. It can be refrigerated for several weeks. In a non-stick pan sauté capsicum, onion and garlic in the oil for about 20 minutes, until capsicum is very soft and onion caramelised, adding sugar and vinegar after 10 minutes. Season with salt and pepper, and cook for another 1–2 minutes, stirring. Allow to cool.

Season whiting fillets and coat with cornflour. Heat oil and butter together in a non-stick pan and gently fry the fish for about 40 seconds on each side, until lightly golden.

Top each piece of buttered toast with capsicum relish and place four whiting fillets on each. Serve at once.

SERVES 2

Pasta squares with pesto & parmesan

4 gluten-free lasagne sheets

salt

1 bunch fresh basil

1 clove garlic

2 tablespoons pine nuts

2 tablespoons grated parmesan cheese

75–100 ml extra-virgin olive oil

shaved parmesan cheese

freshly ground black pepper

Bring a large saucepan of well salted water to the boil and add the lasagne sheets, stirring to prevent them sticking. When water comes back to the boil, reduce heat and simmer for 8–10 minutes, until cooked al dente.

While pasta is cooking, make the fresh pesto by picking leaves from the basil and grinding in a food processor with the garlic, pine nuts, parmesan and a pinch of salt. Slowly add the oil to make a luscious, oily green sauce.

Tip the cooked pasta into a strainer to drain and then cut each sheet in half and layer on plates with a spoonful of the pesto between each layer. Finish with more pesto and a little peak of shaved parmesan and some cracked black pepper.

SERVES 2

Cold buckwheat noodles with chicken, cucumber & sesame

400 g soba (buckwheat) noodles

1 tablespoon sesame oil

1½ cups diced roast chicken

3–4 spring onions, chopped

1 Lebanese cucumber, diced

2 tablespoons tahini

1½ cups chicken stock

salt and freshly ground black pepper

fish sauce or gluten-free soy sauce

8 large well-chilled lettuce leaves, finely shredded

Cook the soba noodles in boiling, lightly salted water for 4–5 minutes until tender. Drain and cool in cold water, then drain thoroughly.

In a bowl toss noodles with sesame oil and then add chicken, spring onions and cucumber, mixing well.

In another bowl combine tahini and chicken stock, beating until creamy and slightly runny. If too thick, add a little more chicken stock or water. Season to taste with salt, pepper and fish or soy sauce.

Gently fold tahini dressing through the noodles and serve over chilled lettuce.

SERVES 4

Dinner

Crumb crusts and stuffing can present problems in a gluten-free diet, but with gluten-free breadcrumbs and batters, potato pie crusts and creative alternatives like buckwheat grains, felafel mix and dukkah adding flavour and crunch, these are dishes the whole family can enjoy together. Entertaining is also easy, with quick cook ideas that are sure to impress.

Curries thickened with ground nuts and coconut cream, plain grills and roasts, and simple steamed fish or chicken are trouble-free choices, and by using fish sauce or a gluten-free soy sauce, stir-fries make a satisfying fast cook meal.

Unless otherwise labelled, commercial gravy mixes contain gluten-based thickening ingredients. But it's easy to make your own gluten-free gravy. Simply boil up your pan juices, scraping the bottom of the pan to loosen any bits of meat, and thicken by slowly stirring in a solution of maize cornflour or arrowroot

< Grilled fish with herb crumbs (page 91)

mixed with cold water, or use a balloon whisk to mix in kneaded butter (made by mashing butter into gluten-free plain flour). Continue to stir until the gravy thickens, then season to taste. Or for a gravy made without pan juices, reduce stock over medium heat to intensify its flavour, then thicken with arrow-root or maize cornflour mixed with cold water.

Grilled fish with herb crumbs

4 pieces fresh fish (snapper, tuna, basa, salmon)

salt and freshly ground black pepper

2 slices gluten-free bread

2–3 sprigs parsley

2–3 sprigs dill

juice and zest of 1 lemon

2–3 tablespoons light olive oil

Trim the fish so it is of even thickness and season with salt and pepper.

In a food processor chop the bread, parsley and dill to crumbs. Add lemon zest and enough oil to moisten and hold crumbs together.

Heat grill to hot, and heat remaining oil in a non-stick pan.

Press crumbs evenly over one side of the fish, and carefully place in the pan crumb-side up. Brown the fish on the underside, cooking for about 2 minutes, and then place the pan under the grill to cook the top.

Squeeze on lemon juice, and serve.

SERVES 4

Salmon on potato pancake with salsa verde

2 salmon steaks

olive oil, for frying

2 medium pink-skinned potatoes

1 tablespoon gluten-free plain flour

1 egg, lightly beaten

salt and freshly ground black pepper

SALSA VERDE

3 large sprigs parsley

12 large basil leaves

2–3 sprigs fresh dill

1 clove garlic

1 anchovy fillet (optional)

2 teaspoons capers, drained

freshly squeezed lemon juice

salt and freshly ground black pepper

6 tablespoons olive oil

Season the fish with salt and pepper and brush or spray with olive oil.

Combine the ingredients for the salsa verde, except the oil, in a food processor or blender and grind to a paste, and then add the olive oil and process briefly.

Peel and coarsely grate the potato and squeeze out as much water as possible. Mix with flour and the beaten egg and divide the mixture in two.

Heat a non-stick pan with a thin film of olive oil and put in the potato mixture, pressing into two flat pancakes. Cook on medium heat for about 3 minutes on each side, and then increase the heat slightly and push to one side to make room for the salmon. Cook salmon for about 1½ minutes on each side, or until done to preference.

When salmon and potato cakes are both cooked, serve onto warmed plates and top generously with the herb sauce. Serve at once.

SERVES 2

Moroccan prawns with chermoula

20 large green prawns,
   in their shells

4—5 sprigs coriander

4—5 sprigs parsley

1—2 cloves garlic

1½ teaspoons ground cumin

1 teaspoon harissa or other hot
   chilli paste

salt and freshly ground black
   pepper

juice of 1 lemon

olive oil, for frying

4 pieces gluten-free flatbread
   (page 241)

½ cup purchased baba ganoush
   dip

50 g small-leaf lettuce and herb
   mix

Shell prawns leaving tails on. Devein cutting deeply along centre back.

In a food processor or blender combine herbs, garlic, cumin, harissa, salt
and pepper and lemon juice and grind to a paste. Mix with the prawns,
cover with plastic wrap and refrigerate for 1 hour.

Cook on a barbecue, hot grill or non-stick pan moistened with a little olive oil.

Warm flatbread, spread with eggplant dip, scatter on lettuce and herbs and
top with the prawns.

SERVES 4

Grilled chicken with herbs under the skin

2 chicken kiev (breast and wing bone)
   or marylands (leg and thigh), skin on

3 tablespoons butter or olive oil

salt and freshly ground black pepper

2 rosemary sprigs

4 thyme sprigs

4 fresh oregano sprigs

2 lemon slices

side salad, to serve

Lift the edge of the skin, of the chicken, and carefully work the handle of a wooden spoon between skin and meat to form a pocket.

Make a paste of butter, salt and pepper, or mix oil with seasonings and spread in the pocket, following with the herb sprigs and a lemon slice. Brush or spray the chicken all over with oil.

Heat a grill to medium and cook the chicken, turning several times, until the skin is golden and crisp and the chicken cooked through (about 8–10 minutes). Serve with a side salad.

SERVES 2

Korma chicken curry

1 small chicken or 1 kg chicken
pieces

salt

2 tablespoons ghee or oil

1 large onion, peeled and
roughly chopped

1–2 cloves garlic

2 thick slices fresh ginger, peeled

1½ teaspoons ground coriander

1½ teaspoons garam masala

⅓ teaspoon ground cinnamon

1 cup cream or sour cream

1 tablespoon sultanas or raisins

1 tablespoon macadamia butter
or finely ground almonds or
macadamias

Cut the chicken into eight pieces, rinse, dry and season with salt. Heat oil or
ghee in a saucepan and brown the chicken, turning several times. Remove to
a plate. Slide saucepan away from heat. Grind onion, garlic and ginger to a
paste in a food processor or blender. Reheat the saucepan and fry the onion
paste for about 2 minutes, stirring often. Add spices, 1 cup water and the
chicken and cover. Bring to the boil, reduce heat to medium and simmer for
20 minutes.

Add cream or sour cream, sultanas or raisins and continue to simmer for a
further 20 minutes on medium-low heat. Check seasoning and stir in the
macadamia butter or ground nuts. Cook gently for about 5 minutes. Serve
with basmati rice and chutney.

SERVES 3–4

Chicken parmigiana

1 chicken breast or 2 veal steaks or schnitzels

salt and freshly ground black pepper

2–3 tablespoons potato starch or cornflour

1 large egg, beaten with 2 tablespoons milk

2 thick slices gluten-free bread, chopped to crumbs

2–3 tablespoons olive oil

2–3 tablespoons butter

¾ cup tomato pasta sauce

3–4 tablespoons grated cheese

Place chicken breast or veal steak flat on a board and cut into two thin slices. Bat each out between plastic sheets to make large, thin schnitzels. Season lightly and coat with potato starch or cornflour, shaking off excess. Dip into beaten egg and coat thickly with crumbs, pressing them on. Set on a plate and refrigerate 20 minutes to 1 hour to firm up the coating.

Heat the grill to hot. Melt butter and oil in a large pan and fry the parmigiana for about 1½ minutes on each side, until crumbs are golden.

Transfer to the grill tray. Spread on tomato sauce and cheese and grill until cheese melts. Serve at once.

MAKES 2

Lamb racks with crunchy herb crust

4 lamb racks, each 3—4 ribs

1 slice gluten-free white bread

2 sprigs parsley

2 sprigs fresh oregano

½ cup rice crumbs

2 tablespoons grated parmesan

grated zest of 1 lemon

salt and freshly ground black pepper

3 tablespoons oil

Preheat the oven to 180°C.

To help crumbs stay in place, score the meat side of the racks with a sharp knife.

Place bread in a food processor with parsley and oregano and chop to crumbs. Add rice crumbs, parmesan, lemon zest and seasoning and use pulse control to mix well. Work in just enough oil to moisten the crumbs so they stick together. Press crumbs evenly over the scored part of the racks, and carefully lift onto a baking tray lined with baking paper.

Roast for 25–30 minutes, until the racks are pink-tender and the crust golden-brown. Remove from the oven and let rest for 3–4 minutes before serving.

SERVES 4

Blue cheese chicken kiev

2 chicken kiev (half-breast with wing bone)

salt and freshly ground black pepper

40–50 g blue cheese

1–2 eggs

2–3 tablespoons gluten-free flour or cornflour

¾ cup rice crumbs

2 cups oil

crisp salad, to serve

Push the blade of a sharp knife into the centre of the kiev to form a pocket for the cheese. Season chicken with salt and pepper and press half the cheese into each kiev.

Beat the egg in a shallow bowl, spread flour in another bowl and crumbs in another. Coat chicken with flour, dip into egg allowing excess to drip off, then coat with crumbs.

Repeat egg and crumb coating, and place chicken in the refrigerator for 1 hour to set. (The chicken can be done in advance, wrapped in plastic and kept overnight.)

Heat the oil in a deep pan to medium-hot and fry the chicken, turning several times, for 6–8 minutes, until golden-brown outside, and tender inside.

Serve at once, with a crisp salad.

 Garlic butter, brie or camembert can replace the blue cheese in this recipe.

SERVES 2

Grilled lamb with dukkah & mint yoghurt

2 × 200 g pieces lamb backstrap
salt and freshly ground black pepper
1½—2 tablespoons dukkah
¾ cup natural yoghurt
5—6 fresh mint leaves (or 2 teaspoons mint sauce)
lettuce mix, to serve

Brush the lamb with olive oil and season with salt and pepper.

Heat a barbecue, hot plate or heavy non-stick pan and put the lamb on to grill for about 3 minutes on each side, turning once.

Serve dukkah into two small dishes. Combine yoghurt with chopped mint leaves or mint sauce.

Let lamb rest for 2–3 minutes after cooking, then place on warmed plates with a dish of dukkah on the side, a wedge of lemon, lettuce, and a generous spoonful of yoghurt on top.

SERVES 2

April 30   · 4/5

Fish in batter

2 large egg whites, well beaten

2 tablespoons rice flour

2 tablespoons cornflour, plus extra for cooking

2 pieces firm white fish

salt and finely ground pepper

a few fennel seeds, crushed (optional)

2 cups oil, for deep frying

In a bowl beat egg whites to soft peaks and fold in the two flours.

Season fish lightly with salt, pepper and fennel seeds (if using) and coat with cornflour, shaking off excess.

Heat oil to medium–hot in a wok or frying pan.

Drag the fish through the batter to coat, turning once or twice.

Carefully slide the fish into the oil to fry for about 3 minutes on each side, until golden-brown and crisp.

Drain and serve at once with the fat 'n' crunchy fries from page 162.

SERVES 2

Creamy fish pie

500 g firm fish (basa, flake, blue eye)

salt and freshly ground black pepper

1 large onion, diced

½ celery stick

1 clove garlic, chopped

2 tablespoons butter

½ teaspoon fennel seeds

2 cups milk

2½ tablespoons cornflour

1 fish stock cube or 1¼ teaspoons fish stock powder

1 cup corn or peas

2–3 tablespoons chopped herbs (parsley and dill)

3 large potatoes, peeled and cubed

2 tablespoons sour cream

1 egg

½ cup grated tasty cheese (optional)

Cut fish into 3-cm cubes and season lightly. Set aside.

Sauté onion, celery and garlic in the butter for two minutes. Add fennel seeds, cover and cook gently for 2 more minutes.

Mix ¼ cup milk with the cornflour and pour remainder over the onion, adding stock cube or powder, corn or peas, and bring to the boil. Simmer for 2 minutes, then stir in cornflour mixture and simmer, stirring, until it begins to thicken (about 2 minutes).

Add the fish and season to taste and cook gently for 2–3 minutes. Stir in herbs.

Preheat oven to 200°C.

In the meantime, boil the potatoes in salted water until tender.

Spread the fish in a shallow oven dish.

Drain potatoes and mash with cream, egg and seasoning and spread evenly over the fish. Scatter on cheese (if using) and bake for about 15 minutes, or until the top is golden-brown.

SERVES 4

Ten-minute Thai red beef curry

1 small carrot, peeled and thinly sliced

1 cup coconut milk

1 teaspoon Thai red curry paste

2 spring onions, sliced

3 button mushrooms, rinsed and sliced

200 g rump steak, thinly sliced

30—40 g canned sliced bamboo shoots, drained

fish sauce

salt and freshly ground black pepper

lemon or lime juice (optional)

Boil carrot in lightly salted water for 3 minutes and drain.

In a small saucepan bring coconut milk and ⅓ cup water to the boil. Stir in curry paste and simmer for about 1 minute. Add onions, carrot and mushrooms and simmer for 2 minutes. Add steak and bamboo shoots, salt and pepper to taste and a generous squirt of fish sauce and simmer for about 1 minute, until steak is very lightly cooked.

Remove from the heat, add lemon or lime juice to taste (if using), and serve with rice.

 This curry is so quick you need to put the rice on to cook before you begin.

SERVES 2

Spicy Middle Eastern meatloaf

90 g felafel mix
½ medium onion, chopped
4–5 parsley sprigs
90 g gluten-free white bread
450 g minced beef or lamb
salt and freshly ground black pepper
4 hardboiled eggs

Preheat the oven to 180°C.

Brush a loaf tin with olive oil. In a bowl combine felafel mix and ½ cup water and leave for about 15 minutes to soften.

Place onion, parsley and bread in a food processor and grind to crumbs. Add mince and mix well, seasoning lightly. Tip onto the felafel paste and mix in well with hands. Spread half in the bottom of the loaf tin.

Shell the eggs, remove a slice from both ends so they sit closely together, and press end to end into the meatloaf mixture. Cover with the remaining mixture, smoothing the top and brushing lightly with olive oil.

Bake uncovered for 40–50 minutes, until the top is firm and brown and the meatloaf is cooked through. Slice thickly to serve hot, or allow to cool, then refrigerate to serve cold.

SERVE 6–8

Vegetarian lasagne

2 zucchinis

1 globe eggplant

olive oil, for frying

salt and freshly ground black
  pepper

1 head broccoli

1 bunch leaf spinach or ½ bunch
  silverbeet

2 cups ricotta cheese

2 cups tomato pasta sauce

1½ cups grated melting cheese

⅓ cup grated parmesan cheese

BÉCHAMEL SAUCE

100 g butter

⅔ cup gluten-free plain flour

1 litre milk

salt and freshly ground black
  pepper

⅔ teaspoon grated nutmeg
  (optional)

To make the béchamel sauce, melt butter in a small saucepan and stir in flour. Cook, stirring with a wire whisk, until it thickens, and then add ¾ cup milk and whisk over medium heat. When smooth add the remaining milk, salt and pepper and whisk gently until the sauce thickens and becomes smooth. Add nutmeg (if using).

Very thinly slice unpeeled zucchinis and eggplant. Heat about 1.5 cm oil in a large pan and fry in batches until lightly browned, then drain on a rack over a tray. Season with salt and pepper and set aside.

Preheat oven to 180°C. >

Thinly slice the broccoli, including the peeled stem. Slice the silverbeet steams and shred the green tops. Bring a pan of lightly salted water to the boil and cook the broccoli and silverbeet stems for 3 minutes, add shredded leaves or spinach and cook for another 1–2 minutes. Tip into a colander to drain thoroughly.

Brush or spray a square baking pan or casserole with olive oil.

Use a third of the zucchini and eggplant to cover the base of the prepared pan and scatter on teaspoons of ricotta cheese, lay over half the broccoli and spinach or silverbeet, add more ricotta cheese and cover with tomato sauce.

Add a second layer of zucchini and eggplant and repeat with the ricotta, broccoli, spinach or silverbeet and tomato sauce and season well.

Layer remaining zucchini and eggplant, cover with béchamel sauce and scatter on the cheeses.

Bake for about 35 minutes, until the cheese is bubbling and golden-brown. Let it sit for a few minutes after removing from the oven. Serve hot or refrigerate until firm enough to cut into squares to serve cold with salad.

SERVES 6–8

Albondigas (Spanish meatballs in tomato sauce)

500 g lean lamb, beef or veal, diced

1 small onion, peeled and cut in half

1 clove garlic

3–4 sprigs parsley

½ teaspoon dried oregano

1 teaspoon smoked paprika

1¼ teaspoons salt

freshly ground black pepper

1 egg, beaten

½ cup potato starch or gluten-free breadcrumbs

1 cup olive oil

2 cups bottled tomato sauce (passata or pasta sauce)

Place meat in a food processor and grind smooth. Remove to a bowl.

Add onion, garlic and parsley to the processor and grind well, then add oregano, paprika, salt, pepper and egg and return the meat. Grind until very well pulverised and thoroughly mixed together. With wet hands form into twenty-four meatballs and coat with potato starch.

Heat oil in a non-stick pan and cook the meatballs over medium heat until browned on all sides, and cooked through (about 6 minutes). Remove the meatballs to a plate covered with paper towels to drain.

Pour off oil, wipe out the pan and add the tomato sauce. Return the meatballs and simmer in the sauce for 3–4 minutes. Serve hot.

MAKES 24 (SERVES 4–6)

Cauliflower, broccoli & potato bake

300 g cauliflower

250 g broccoli or 200 g chopped cabbage

4–5 small potatoes

salt and freshly ground black pepper

2 tablespoons butter

1 medium onion, finely chopped

1 clove garlic, chopped

2 cups cheese sauce (page 50)

¼–⅓ cup grated parmesan or gluten-free bread
   crumbs, or 2 tablespoons polenta (optional)

Preheat oven to 220°C.

Cut cauliflower and broccoli into small florets. Slice potatoes and place in a pot of salted water to boil for about 8 minutes. Separately cook cauliflower and broccoli or cabbage in lightly salted water for about 5 minutes until almost tender.

Thickly butter a large oven dish and set aside.

In a small pan sauté the onion and garlic in butter until translucent. **>**

Line the oven dish with drained potato slices, cover with sautéed onion and season well. Top with the cauliflower and broccoli or cabbage. Spread cheese sauce over the vegetables and sprinkle over parmesan, crumbs or polenta (if using). Bake for about 20 minutes until the top is golden-brown.

SERVES 4 AS A MAIN COURSE, OR 6–8 AS A SIDE DISH

Chilli con carne

500 g minced lamb or beef
1 medium onion, finely diced
2 cloves garlic, finely chopped
½ celery stick, finely chopped
½ red capsicum, finely chopped
2 tablespoons olive oil
1½ teaspoons ground cumin
½ teaspoon ground cinnamon
2½ teaspoons paprika
1 teaspoon soft brown sugar
1–2 teaspoons finely chopped
  red chilli

salt and freshly ground black
  pepper
1 teaspoon dried oregano, or
  1 tablespoon chopped fresh
  oregano
1 × 410-g can crushed tomatoes
1 × 400-g can kidney beans,
  drained
1 × 425-g can bean mix, drained
½ cup fresh, canned or frozen
  corn kernels

Sauté mince, onion, garlic, celery and capsicum in oil for about 10 minutes, stirring frequently. Add spices, sugar, chilli, seasoning and oregano and cook briefly. Stir in tomatoes and 1 cup water and simmer until the liquid has almost evaporated and the mince is tender (about 10 minutes).

Add beans and corn and cook gently for a few minutes, adding water if needed. Check seasoning. Serve on its own, with tortillas or rice.

SERVES 4–5

Risotto of prawns & pumpkin

250 g peeled pumpkin, diced

1 medium onion, finely diced

2 cloves garlic, diced

2 tablespoons olive oil

1½ cups risotto rice (arborio)

2 teaspoons chicken or vegetable stock powder

6 cups boiling water

215 g small peeled prawns

1½ cups grated tasty cheese

salt and freshly ground black pepper

2–3 tablespoons chopped fresh herbs (parsley and basil or dill)

Sauté pumpkin, onion and garlic in a frying pan with oil until lightly browned (about 4 minutes).

Add rice and stir to coat with oil. Stir stock powder into the boiling water and slowly add to the rice, ¾ cup at a time, stirring and not adding more until the previous liquid is absorbed. When all is absorbed the risotto should still be moist and slightly soupy, while the rice is tender but al dente. Add the prawns and cook for 1–2 minutes, then stir in cheese, season to taste and add herbs.

Serve in shallow bowls.

SERVES 4–5

Crumbed pork tonkatsu

4 pork schnitzels

salt and freshly ground black pepper

½ cup cornflour

1–2 eggs

1½ cups rice crumbs

1½ cups medium grain white rice

1 large onion, finely sliced

oil, for shallow frying

TONKATSU SAUCE

3 tablespoons tomato sauce

1 tablespoon Worcestershire sauce

1 tablespoon gluten-free soy sauce (or fish sauce)

1 tablespoon gluten-free oyster sauce

One at a time, place schnitzels between two pieces of plastic wrap and bat with a meat mallet or rolling pin to flatten out to about .7 cm thick.

Season with salt and pepper and coat lightly with cornflour. Beat eggs in a shallow dish and spread rice crumbs in another. Dip schnitzels in egg, and then coat with crumbs. Refrigerate for 20 minutes to set.

Pour 2½ cups water over the rice in a medium-sized saucepan and cover. Bring to the boil, reduce heat to very low and simmer without opening the pan, for about 12 minutes until the water is absorbed and the rice tender and dry. ➤

In 1½ tablespoons oil sauté the onion until tender and browned (about 7 minutes).

Mix the sauce ingredients together in a bowl and set aside.

Heat about 4 cm oil in a large pan and fry the schnitzels two at a time for about 2½ minutes on each side, or until golden-brown and cooked through. Keep warm while the remaining two are cooked.

Serve rice into deep bowls, top with onions, thickly sliced pork and the sauce.

SERVES 4

Cajun rice jambalaya

1 gluten-free chorizo sausage, or 120 g salami, sliced

1 celery stick, chopped

1 medium onion, chopped

2 cloves garlic, chopped

2 tablespoons oil

1 green capsicum, diced

1 red capsicum, diced

1½ cups long grain rice

410-g can crushed tomatoes

1 cup (170 g) small peeled prawns

1 teaspoon sambal ulek or crushed chilli

salt and freshly ground black pepper

2–3 tablespoons chopped fresh herbs (a mix of parsley and dill or basil), extra for garnish

In a saucepan with a heavy base fry the chorizo or salami, celery, onion, garlic and capsicum in the oil for about 6 minutes, stirring frequently.

Add rice and cook over high heat for 1 minute.

Pour in tomatoes and 1½ cups water and simmer, stirring occasionally, over medium heat for about 10 minutes, or until the rice is almost tender and the liquid well reduced. Add prawns and chilli and season to taste with salt and pepper. Cover and cook until the rice is tender and prawns pink (about 5 minutes). Stir, adding 2–3 tablespoons herbs.

Transfer to deep bowls and garnish with extra herbs.

SERVES 4

Steamed rice sheets with prawns & cha siu pork

½ pack rice sheets
170 g small peeled green prawns
white pepper
a few sprigs coriander
150 g cha siu roast pork, sliced
gluten-free soy sauce, to serve

Place the wrapped rice sheets in a steamer for a few minutes to soften enough to unwrap without tearing. Unwrap and cut into 12-cm × 18-cm rectangles and brush lightly with sesame oil.

Place ¼ cup prawns along the centre of four sheets, add a sprig of coriander to each and dust with pepper. Roll up and place on a plate in the steamer.

Place sliced pork along the centre of the other sheets, roll up and place on another plate in the steamer.

Scatter a few sprigs of coriander over the top, add a sprinkle of sesame oil and about 1 tablespoon soy sauce.

Cover and steam for about 12 minutes until the prawns are pink and the rice sheets very tender and moist.

Drizzle on extra soy sauce, and serve.

Ready-to-use rice sheets can be found in the chiller section of most Asian food stores. The sheets can be used whole, as in this recipe, or sliced into ribbon noodles. They will keep fresh in the fridge for up to 1 week.

SERVES 3—4

Rice vermicelli with grilled steak & hoisin-peanut sauce

½ pack rice vermicelli

2 thin grilling steaks

½ teaspoon crushed ginger

1½ tablespoons oil

salt and freshly ground black pepper

1 spring onion, finely chopped

2 tablespoons hoisin sauce

2 teaspoons fish sauce

2–3 teaspoons chopped roasted peanuts

½ teaspoon chopped fresh red chilli

Soften the vermicelli in warm water for 5–6 minutes, and drain thoroughly.

Combine ginger, oil, salt and pepper and brush over the steaks. Cook on a hot grill until lightly browned and cooked through, 2½–3½ minutes on each side.

Mix chopped spring onion with any remaining marinade and stir through the vermicelli. Mound on two plates, place a sliced steak on top.

In a small bowl combine the hoisin, fish sauce, peanuts and chilli to make a sauce. Spoon over the steak and noodles and serve at once.

SERVES 2

Pad Thai

375 g rice stick noodles

1 tablespoon soft brown sugar

¼ cup fish sauce

1½ tablespoons tomato sauce

2 tablespoons sweet chilli sauce

3 tablespoons oil

2 spring onions, sliced

2 large cloves garlic, chopped

1½ cups small cooked prawns

1½ cups fresh bean sprouts

2 tablespoons chopped roasted peanuts

2–3 tablespoons garlic chives, sliced

Soak noodles in hot water for 6–7 minutes to soften, and drain well.

In a bowl mix sugar, fish sauce, tomato sauce and sweet chilli.

Heat the oil in a wok and stir-fry garlic and spring onions for about 30 seconds. Add the noodles and fish sauce mix and toss energetically in the wok to coat.

Add prawns, bean sprouts and half the peanuts and stir-fry for about 1 minute.

Serve onto plates or into shallow bowls, garnishing with remaining peanuts and the garlic chives.

SERVES 3–4

Singapore spicy rice vermicelli

200 g fine rice vermicelli

1 medium onion, finely sliced

½ red capsicum, cut into fine strips

150 g chicken breast, cut into shreds

2 tablespoons oil

1–1½ tablespoons mild curry powder

1–2 pieces stem ginger in syrup, finely chopped

¾ cup (155 g) small cooked prawns

1 cup (100 g) fresh bean sprouts

salt and freshly ground black pepper

fish sauce or gluten-free soy sauce

coriander sprigs, to garnish

Soak vermicelli in boiling water to soften and then drain well.

Heat a wok and stir-fry the onion, capsicum and chicken in the oil until the chicken is cooked and the capsicum and onion are soft (about 2½ minutes).

Add the curry powder, ginger, prawns and bean sprouts and stir together over high heat for 1 minute.

Add vermicelli and toss until everything is well mixed.

Season to taste with fish or soy sauce, salt and pepper and serve garnished with coriander.

SERVES 3–4

Pasta with peas & bacon in cheese sauce

1 × 250-g packet corn and
spinach pasta shells or tubes

salt

¾ cup peas

2 slices bacon, diced

1 small onion, diced

3½ cups milk

3 tablespoons cornflour

1 cup grated tasty cheese

freshly ground black pepper

grated parmesan cheese, to serve

Bring a saucepan of salted water to the boil and cook pasta for 8 minutes. Add peas and cook until pasta and peas are tender (2–3 minutes). Drain.

In the meantime fry the bacon and onion in a saucepan without oil, until cooked (about 4 minutes).

Stir cornflour into 1 cup milk. Pour remaining milk into the saucepan and bring to the boil. Add cornflour milk and stir until it comes to the boil, and then simmer, stirring frequently, until thickened.

Add cheese and season to taste, and then stir in the drained pasta and peas, mix in well and serve garnished with grated parmesan.

SERVES 2–4

Chicken & spinach pasta bake

180 g frozen spinach

250 g gluten-free macaroni

salt and freshly ground black
  pepper

2 cups milk

2 tablespoons cornflour

2 teaspoons chicken (or
  vegetable) stock powder

¼ teaspoon ground nutmeg

300 g cooked chicken (about
  ½ large roast chicken)

1½ cups grated tasty cheese

½ cup gluten-free fresh
  breadcrumbs (optional)

Preheat the oven to 200°C.

Thaw spinach in the microwave for about 2 minutes on high, and set aside.

Heat a saucepan of salted water and boil pasta according to pack
directions (about 10 minutes). Drain well.

In the meantime, mix milk, cornflour, stock powder and nutmeg in a small
saucepan and bring to the boil, stirring continually. Reduce heat and simmer
until thickened, seasoning generously with salt and pepper. Stir in spinach.

Lightly grease or oil a casserole dish and spread the drained pasta evenly.

Tear or cut chicken into cubes, discarding skin. Scatter over pasta and stir
through, then cover with the spinach sauce.

Scatter cheese and crumbs (if using) evenly over the top, drizzle with a little oil or a few tiny cubes of butter and place in the oven. Cook for about 25 minutes, until the top is golden-brown.

 For a vegetarian bake, substitute 100 g diced fetta and 200 g ricotta cheese for the chicken.

SERVES 3−4

Fettuccine with beef stroganoff

500 g rump beef, cut into strips

salt and freshly ground black pepper

2 tablespoons gluten-free plain flour

1 medium onion, sliced

2 tablespoons butter

2 tablespoons oil

1½ cups mushrooms, sliced

1 tablespoon tomato paste

⅔ cup sour cream

250 g gluten-free fettuccine

chopped fresh parsley, for garnish

Season beef lightly and coat evenly and lightly with flour. Set aside.

Heat half the butter and oil in a saucepan. Fry onions until soft and translucent, (5 minutes) on medium heat. Add mushrooms and cook until softened. Remove mushrooms and onions to a plate. Add remaining butter and oil and sauté beef until lightly browned. Return mushrooms and onions and add tomato paste, sour cream and salt and pepper to taste. Simmer for a few minutes, then remove from heat, cover and let sit for a few minutes.

Cook fettuccine in salted water to al dente (about 11 minutes). Serve stroganoff with fettuccine on the side, garnished with parsley.

 For mushroom stroganoff use 2–3 punnets of mixed mushrooms instead of beef.

SERVES 3–4

Potato gnocchi

1 kg floury potatoes
½ cup gluten-free plain flour, plus extra if needed
2 egg yolks
salt and freshly ground black pepper

Boil unpeeled potatoes until tender. Drain and peel.

Press potatoes through a ricer or mash by hand until smooth. Do not purée in a food processor or use a stick mixer as this alters the texture and can make the gnocchi tough.

Tip potato onto a board and work in the flour, then make a well in the centre and add the egg yolks, salt and pepper. Work into a smooth, firm dough, adding a little extra flour or egg, as needed.

Knead lightly and roll into a long thin sausage shape.

With a sharp knife cut into 3-cm pieces and press each piece onto the back of a fork, to indent.

Bring a large saucepan of salted water to the boil and cook gnocchi, twelve pieces at a time to prevent them sticking together.

When they rise to the surface, after about 3 minutes, remove with a slotted spoon.

Serve with parmesan or crumbled blue cheese, with tomato sauce and chopped basil, or with fresh sage leaves fried crisp in butter, allowing butter to cook to a nutty brown.

 Ready-made gnocchi is never as silky and tender as this homemade version, however it is a handy standby requiring only a few minutes to cook.

SERVES 4–6

Prawns & bean threads cooked in a clay pot

12 large prawns in their shells

100 g bean thread vermicelli

3 spring onions, chopped

5 thin slices fresh ginger, finely shredded

¼ cup tomato pasta sauce

3 tablespoons fish sauce

1 tablespoon mirin or rice wine (optional)

2–3 tablespoons sweet chilli sauce

gluten-free soy sauce, to serve

Preheat oven to 180°C.

Rinse and drain whole unshelled prawns.

Soak vermicelli in hot water for 5–6 minutes to soften, and drain.

Spread the vermicelli in the bottom of a clay pot or oven dish and arrange prawns, onions and ginger over the top. Mix tomato sauce with 2 cups water, the fish sauce, mirin or rice wine (if using) and sweet chilli and pour into the dish.

Cover and place in the oven to cook for about 30 minutes (or cook uncovered in a steamer for 15–20 minutes).

Serve with a splash of soy sauce.

SERVES 3–4

Pasta with blue cheese & pine nuts

200 g gluten-free spaghetti or fettuccine

2 tablespoons butter or light olive oil

1 small onion, finely chopped

1½ tablespoons pine nuts

¾ cup cream

salt and black pepper

120 g gorgonzola or other blue cheese, crumbled

chopped fresh parsley or basil

a handful of rocket or baby spinach leaves (optional)

1–2 tablespoons grated parmesan cheese (optional)

Add pasta to a saucepan of well salted simmering water and leave to cook for about 9 minutes, to al dente.

Heat butter or oil in a sauté pan and sauté onion until lightly coloured. Add pine nuts and continue to sauté until golden-brown. Pour in cream and add salt and pepper. When warmed through add the cheese and a few teaspoons of chopped herbs and cook gently to melt cheese.

With tongs transfer cooked pasta to the pan, add the rocket or spinach and parmesan (if using), and toss to mix well.

Serve into shallow bowls.

SERVES 2

Polenta, eggplant & tomato bake

½ recipe soft polenta (page 170)

2 tablespoons olive oil

½ cup tomato and basil pasta sauce

1 small globe eggplant, diced

½ green capsicum, diced

½ medium onion, diced

½ cup grated parmesan cheese

Preheat the oven to 200°C.

Brush a square oven dish or lasagne dish with olive oil and spread the polenta to 2–3 cm thickness. Pour tomato pasta sauce evenly over and set aside.

In the remaining oil sauté eggplant, capsicum and onion for about 4 minutes, until softened. Spread over the polenta and sprinkle on parmesan.

Bake for 15–20 minutes and serve hot.

 Try a salad of wild rocket and shaved zucchini in a creamy Caesar sauce as a side dish for this vegetarian meal.

SERVES 4

Chinese pork cabbage rolls on rice

500 g pork mince

1 tablespoon gluten-free soy or fish sauce

2 teaspoons rice wine

½ teaspoon ground star anise

½ teaspoon five spice

½ teaspoon salt

½ small Chinese cabbage (wombok)

1¾ cups medium grain white rice

3 cups chicken stock or water

3 thin slices fresh ginger, shredded

2 spring onions, finely sliced

Place mince, soy or fish sauce, rice wine, spices and salt in a food processor and grind to a smooth paste. With wet hands form into 18–20 balls.

Separate the cabbage leaves and select 18–20 pieces. Cut off thick white stem end, leaving the soft crinkly top part of the leaves. Blanch briefly in boiling water and drain. Wrap each meatball in a cabbage leaf and set aside.

Pour rice into a saucepan and add water or stock. Cover and bring to the boil, and then reduce heat to very low and simmer for 5 minutes. Arrange cabbage rolls over the rice and scatter on ginger and onions.

Cover and continue to cook on low heat for about 12 minutes without lifting the lid. Remove from the heat and let rest, tightly covered, for another 5–6 minutes before serving.

SERVES 4

Scallops in spicy peanut sauce

12 large fresh sea scallops on the shell

2 teaspoons oil

2 tablespoons smooth peanut butter

¾ teaspoon Thai red curry paste

½ cup coconut cream

2–3 teaspoons kecap manis (sweet soy sauce)

salt and freshly ground black pepper

chopped spring-onion greens or coriander,
   to serve

Loosen the scallops by running a knife under them. Sprinkle with oil and place under a hot grill for about 3 minutes to cook.

In a small saucepan gently heat the peanut butter with curry paste and coconut cream, to make a smooth thick sauce. Add half the kecap manis and salt and pepper to taste and spoon over the scallops. Finish with a few extra drops of kecap manis and some chopped herbs, and serve at once.

Scallops can be served with a small spoon as party food, or as a starter or main with an Asian salad of small leaves, coriander, bean sprouts and grated carrot in a lime juice dressing.

SERVES 2–4

Roast duck on noodles with ginger & Chinese greens

2 teaspoons sesame oil

250 g fresh rice noodles

½ Chinese roast duck

4 baby bok choy or pak choy

3 thin slices fresh ginger, very finely shredded

2 tablespoons honey soy marinade or hoisin sauce

Place a piece of baking paper in one basket of a stacked Chinese steamer and pierce in several places with a sharp skewer. Brush lightly with sesame oil. Spread the noodles over the paper and sprinkle on extra sesame oil.

Cut the duck into four pieces and place into another basket of the steamer, along with the rinsed and drained vegetables. Scatter ginger on top.

Cover and steam for about 10 minutes, until noodles are hot and tender, the duck warmed through and the vegetables softly wilted.

Spread noodles in shallow bowls, top with greens and ginger and the duck.

Finish with honey soy marinade or hoisin sauce, and serve.

 With Chinese roast meat shops accessible in most cities, roast duck and pork (cha siu) make fabulously tasty easy meals.

SERVES 2–4

Lamb cutlets with char-grilled artichokes

12 French trimmed lamb cutlets

salt and freshly ground black
  pepper

12 marinated or canned
  artichokes

3 teaspoons seeded mustard

3 tablespoons cream

1½ tablespoons chopped flat leaf
  parsley

Brush lamb lightly with oil and add seasoning. Place on a hot grill, barbecue or heavy iron pan to cook for about 2½ minutes on each side.

Place half the artichokes in a food processor. Process to a coarse paste adding the mustard, parsley and cream, and a hint of salt and pepper.

Slice the remainder of the artichokes and brush or spray with olive oil. Lightly brown them on a hot plate or non-stick pan, or on the barbecue beside the lamb cutlets.

Gently heat the artichoke cream in a non-stick pan or microwave oven.

To serve, arrange lamb on individual plates, add a spoonful of the creamed artichokes and one or two slices of the grilled artichokes.

 This dish can also be served with potatoes roasted with sprigs of rosemary.

SERVES 4

Mussels in creamy wine sauce

2 kg black lip mussels in their
  shells

fennel *garlic* { 1 spring-onion greens

1 parsley sprig

3-cm piece celery and a few
  leaves

1 tablespoon butter or oil

1 cup dry white wine

salt and freshly ground black
  pepper

½ cup cream

fresh coriander or flat leaf
  parsley, chopped

Scrub mussel shells and pull off beards, if needed. Finely chop onion, parsley and celery. In a large saucepan with a tight-fitting lid sauté onion, parsley and celery in butter or oil.

Add mussels to the saucepan and the wine, salt and pepper. Cover tightly and steam, shaking the pan to encourage the shells to open. Check after about 3 minutes, and continue to shake the pan and keep the lid tightly in place so the mussels open as fast as possible. Add the cream and herbs and cook very briefly. Serve in large bowls.

 Add a pinch of saffron threads to the pot for extra flavour.

SERVES 4 OR MORE

Soups, salads & sides

Soup is a satisfying snack. Add crunch and texture with a garnish of toasted tortilla chips, parsley or basil leaves.

Roast vegetables can be jazzed up with herbs, anchovies and balsamic vinegar, steamed and boiled veggies with golden fried pine nuts, cashews and gluten-free crumbs. Vegetable bakes can be dressed with rice crumbs, crushed corn chips, melting cheese and parmesan. Wheat based sides like couscous and cracked wheat can be replaced by quinoa and creamy or grilled polenta.

Salads offer plenty of variety, and pasta or bread components can easily be substituted with gluten-free options such as vegetable pasta, rice vermicelli, buckwheat noodles and bean threads. Croutons made from stale gluten-free bread and flatbread work well in Mediterranean-style bread salads.

< Potato & sweet potato crisps
(page 158)

Potato & sweet potato crisps

2 large floury potatoes, such as Coliban
  or Sebago, or 1 golden sweet potato
1 litre oil, for frying
salt or seasoned (chicken) salt

Peel the potatoes and use a mandolin, knife or potato peeler to shave into very thin slices. Rinse in cold water, drain and dry by shaking in a kitchen cloth.

Heat the oil to 170°C, and have ready a rack on a tray lined with paper towels, for draining.

Add half the sliced potatoes and slowly stir in the oil using a wooden spoon, to ensure they do not stick together. Cook until golden-brown – listen for a rustling sound as you stir – and then remove with a strainer or perforated spoon and drain on the rack for 1–2 minutes. Sweet potato will cook faster than white potato.

Place remaining slices in the oil to cook, and while the first batch is still warm, season with salt and serve at once, or leave to cool.

Can be stored in an airtight container for 2–3 days.

SERVES 4

Potato galettes

2 medium-sized Pontiac potatoes
½ cup olive oil
salt and freshly ground black pepper

Peel the potatoes and cut into thin slices. Do not rinse as you need the surface starch to help stick the slices together.

Make four rounds of overlapped potato slices.

Heat the oil in a large non-stick pan and carefully lift the potato galettes into the oil on a wide spatula to fry on medium-high heat until golden-brown.

Turn carefully to cook the other side. Lift out and drain briefly on paper towels before serving.

Top these crisp-fried potatoes with a small-leaf salad as a vegetarian first course, or serve beside or beneath grilled meat or fish.

MAKES 4

Grilled tomatoes with herb parmesan crust

4 medium-sized ripe round tomatoes

salt and freshly ground black pepper

1 teaspoon dried thyme

2 tablespoons grated parmesan cheese

2 tablespoons polenta or fresh gluten-free
breadcrumbs

1 tablespoon chopped parsley (optional)

Heat the grill to medium–high.

Cut tomatoes in half and place on a grill tray, cut sides up. Season with salt, pepper and thyme.

Combine parmesan, polenta or crumbs and parsley (if using) and spread evenly over the tomatoes.

Drizzle lightly with olive oil and place under the grill to cook until the tops are golden-brown and the tomatoes soft but not collapsing (about 7 minutes).

SERVES 4

Fat 'n' crunchy fries

4 large floury potatoes, such as Coliban
  or Sebago

salt

½ cup gluten-free plain flour

½ cup gluten-free beer

4–6 cups oil, for frying

Peel the potatoes, cut into large, thin chips and rinse in cold water.

Bring a pot of lightly salted water to the boil and cook chips for about
6 minutes. Drain well and then spread on a tray to dry.

In a large bowl whisk flour, beer and enough cold water to make a runny
batter, the consistency of thin cream.

Heat oil to 160°C in a wok, deep-fryer or large saucepan. Dip chips into
the batter, drain off excess and place in the oil taking care not to overcrowd
the pan. You may need to cook in several batches. Fry until lightly golden,
and then remove with a strainer or slotted spoon and drain on a rack over
paper towels.

Just before the fries are to be served, reheat the oil to 175°C and fry the
chips until golden and crunchy. Drain, season with salt and serve at once.

SERVES 4

Silverbeet with fried pine nuts & currants

½ bunch silverbeet or 1–2 bunches
  English spinach
2½ tablespoons sultanas or currants
2 tablespoons pine nuts
2–3 tablespoons olive oil
salt and freshly ground black pepper

Trim away white ribs from silverbeet leaves and slice them thinly. Place in a pot of salted water to boil for 2–3 minutes.

Finely shred the silverbeet leaves or tear larger spinach leaves in half and add to the saucepan. Cook for about 1 minute, and then drain well.

Heat 2–3 tablespoons oil in a large frying pan or wok and add the sultanas or currants and pine nuts.

Sauté until the fruit is plump and round and the nuts golden (2–3 minutes) on medium heat.

Add the silverbeet or spinach and stir in the oil until well mixed. Season to taste and serve.

SERVES 4

Not-quite couscous

1½ cups quinoa

salt and freshly ground black
  pepper

1 large tomato, seeded and finely
  diced

¼ green capsicum, finely diced

2 spring onions, sliced

4 tablespoons extra-virgin
  olive oil

2 tablespoons chopped raisins

2 tablespoons slivered almonds
  or pine nuts

2 tablespoons chopped mixed
  herbs (parsley, basil, mint,
  coriander)

freshly squeezed lemon juice

Bring a pot of salted water or chicken/vegetable stock to the boil and
simmer quinoa for 10–15 minutes until swollen and tender. Drain well.

Sauté the tomato, capsicum and onion in half the oil until tender. Add
raisins and nuts and cook for a few minutes, stirring.

Add the quinoa, herbs, salt, pepper, the remaining olive oil and lemon
juice to taste and gently warm through.

To serve as a salad, simply let the quinoa cool and mix with the same
ingredients, uncooked. ➤

Quinoa (pronounced 'keen-wa') is an ancient grain which becomes translucent when cooked, and has a bland taste and the texture of caviar. It can be eaten warm as a side dish replacing couscous or rice, or cooled and made into a salad.

SERVES 4

Caesar salad

2 thick slices gluten-free bread

1 cup olive oil

2 cloves garlic, sliced

2 slices bacon, rind removed

2 × little gem cos lettuce, or
  1 large cos

4 anchovy fillets, halved
  lengthwise (optional)

½ cup shaved parmesan cheese

3–4 tablespoons bottled Caesar
  dressing

Trim crusts from bread and cut into 3-cm cubes.

Heat oil in a wok or frying pan over medium-high heat and add the garlic
and bread. Fry until bread is golden-brown, then remove with a slotted
spoon and drain over paper towels.

Pour oil into a container and reheat the pan.

Slice the bacon and fry until crisp, set aside.

Separate lettuce, rinse and spin dry. Discard coarse outer leaves and tear
or slice lettuce, leaving small leaves whole.

Place in 2–4 bowls and add to each some of the croutons, bacon, anchovies
(if using) and parmesan, drizzle on dressing and serve.

SERVES 2–4

Buckwheat tabbouleh

1⅓ cups hulled buckwheat (or use coarse cornmeal, hulled millet or quinoa)

2 cups boiling water

2 tomatoes, seeded and finely chopped

1 large bunch parsley, finely chopped

4–5 mint sprigs, chopped

1 medium red salad onion, finely chopped

3 tablespoons light olive oil

2 tablespoons lemon juice

salt and freshly ground black pepper

Place buckwheat in a food processor or blender and grind using the pulse control, until cracked. Tip into a bowl and pour on the boiling water. Cover and set aside for about 25 minutes, to soften.

In a bowl combine the well drained buckwheat with remaining ingredients, mixing well. Chill before serving.

SERVES 4–6

Soft polenta

1 teaspoon salt

¾ cup (125 g) fine cornmeal (polenta)

2—4 tablespoons butter or olive oil

2—3 tablespoons milk or cream

finely grated parmesan, or other
  cheese (optional)

chopped fresh herbs (optional)

Add salt to a litre of water and bring to the boil and sprinkle in the polenta, whisking energetically to prevent it clumping. Continue to whisk as the water comes back to the boil, and then reduce heat and simmer, stirring frequently, until it becomes thick and creamy and no longer tastes gritty (about 20 minutes).

Whisk in butter or olive oil and milk or cream to give the desired consistency, adding cheese and herbs to taste (if using).

Polenta (fine cornmeal) is an invaluable standby in the gluten-free diet. It can replace semolina in most recipes, including bread, muffins, cakes and puddings, can be enjoyed as a breakfast porridge, makes simply scrumptious bread (page 239), and is a creamy alternative to mashed potatoes.

To make grilled polenta or fried polenta crisps, cook polenta as previously described, but using just 3 cups water and cooking until it is so thick it leaves the sides of the saucepan. To grill, spread in a flat dish brushed with olive oil, cover and refrigerate for several hours or overnight, until firm. Cut into pieces, brush with oil and cook under a very hot grill or in a hot non-stick or cast-iron pan, until golden on the surface. To make fried polenta crisps, cut the polenta into small squares or slices and deep-fry until, crisp and golden.

SERVES 4−6

Bean thread salad of chicken, prawns & nuts

150 g bean thread vermicelli

100 g chicken breast, cut into thin strips

18–20 medium-sized prawns, shelled and deveined

1 tablespoon light olive or peanut oil

salt and freshly ground black pepper

juice of 2 limes or 1 large lemon

2 tablespoons sweet chilli sauce

2 tablespoons soft brown sugar

2 tablespoons fish sauce

1 large red salad onion, finely sliced

2 spring onions, sliced at an angle

1½ cups bean sprouts, blanched and drained

½ green capsicum or seeded cucumber, cut into fine strips

1 large mild red chilli, finely sliced

1 celery stem, finely sliced on a diagonal

⅓ cup roasted peanuts, cashews or macadamias

⅔ cup small herb sprigs (coriander, basil, mint, etc.)

Soak bean threads in boiling water for 1–2 minutes to soften, and drain well.

Stir-fry chicken and prawns in 1 tablespoon oil until cooked (about 2 minutes), season lightly with salt and pepper and set aside in a bowl.

In another bowl whisk lime or lemon juice, sweet chilli, sugar and fish sauce and pour half over the chicken and prawns, stirring in. Set remainder aside. ❯

In a salad bowl combine the onions, bean sprouts, capsicum or cucumber, chilli and celery and toss well.

With kitchen scissors cut through the clump of softened noodles. Mix through the salad adding the nuts, herbs and remaining dressing.

Fold through the chicken and prawns and serve.

 Cooked buckwheat noodles or softened rice vermicelli can replace the bean threads.

SERVES 4−6

Chickpea, tomato & crumbled cornbread salad

1 × 400-g can chickpeas, drained

2 Roma tomatoes, seeded and diced

1 medium salad onion, finely chopped

1 celery stalk, chopped

2 tablespoons extra-virgin olive oil

a big squeeze of lemon juice

salt and freshly ground black pepper

2 slices cornbread (page 239)

8–12 kalamata olives in oil, drained

2–3 sprigs fresh basil, coriander or parsley

Place chickpeas, tomatoes, onion and celery in a salad bowl. Add oil, lemon juice, salt and pepper and toss well.

Toast or grill the cornbread until lightly coloured, and break into pieces.

Scatter cornbread, olives and torn herbs over the salad and serve at once.

SERVES 2–3

Grilled beef salad with green beans, semi-dried tomatoes & garlic toast

1 sirloin steak

2 cloves garlic

salt and freshly ground black
    pepper

½ teaspoon ground cumin

4–6 teaspoons butter or olive oil

2 thin slices gluten-free white
    bread

18 green beans

50 g mesclun lettuce

10 pieces semi-dried tomatoes

4 marinated artichokes, cut in
    half

⅓ cup pitted black olives

2 hardboiled eggs, cut in half

3 tablespoons fruity olive oil

3 teaspoons balsamic vinegar

Trim the steak of excess fat. Mash the garlic with salt and in a small bowl mix half with some freshly ground pepper, the cumin and 2–3 teaspoons butter or oil. Spread over the steak and set on a hot grill.

Mash the remaining garlic with another 2–3 teaspoons butter or oil and spread over the bread. Place on the grill to toast.

Parboil beans in lightly salted water, and drain well.

On two plates assemble mesclun, beans, semi-dried tomatoes, artichokes, olives and eggs.

Whisk olive oil and balsamic vinegar, adding salt and pepper to taste. Pour a little over each salad. >

Remove cooked steak from the heat and let rest for 2–3 minutes, and cut into thin slices.

Drape meat over the salad and finish with the remaining dressing. Add garlic toast and serve.

SERVES 2

Thai pumpkin soup with coconut & ginger

6 cups peeled and diced pumpkin

1 stem lemongrass, cut into chunks

1 x 400-ml can coconut cream

salt or fish sauce, and freshly ground
   black pepper

freshly squeezed lime juice, to taste

4 thin slices fresh ginger, peeled and
   very finely shredded

Place pumpkin in a saucepan with 2 cups water and the lemongrass. Cover and bring to the boil, and then reduce heat and simmer until the pumpkin is very tender (about 12 minutes).

Remove from the heat after it cools for a few minutes remove the lemongrass chunks and use a stick mixer to process to a smooth purée.

Add coconut cream, reserving a little for garnish, salt and/or fish sauce and pepper to taste and simmer gently for 2–3 minutes. Squeeze in a little lime juice and serve into soup bowls.

Garnish with ginger shreds, a swirl of coconut cream and serve.

SERVES 4–6

Chicken noodle soup

1 fresh chicken

1 small onion, quartered

1 small carrot, sliced

½ celery stick, sliced

2 bay leaves

2–3 sprigs fresh thyme

1 cup rice chips, broken rice noodles, or gluten-free short or long pasta

2 spring onions, sliced

salt and freshly ground black pepper

Rinse and drain the chicken and place whole in a large saucepan with 8 cups water, onion, carrot, celery, bay leaves and thyme.

Bring slowly to the boil, skimming occasionally, and then reduce heat and gently simmer for 30 minutes. The water should barely break a bubble as it simmers.

Remove from heat and let sit for 20 minutes to partially cool.

Lift out the chicken and remove the legs and thighs. Skin and debone, and tear the meat into strips. Save breast meat to serve cold, or use in another recipe.

Strain the stock into a clean saucepan and return to the boil, simmering to reduce and condense its flavour. Season to taste with salt and pepper. >

Soften the rice chips or rice noodles in boiling water for 4 minutes, and drain or boil short or long pasta in salted water until just tender (about 7 minutes), drain.

Add drained pasta, chicken and spring onions to the soup and simmer briefly. Check seasoning before serving.

 You could, of course, cut corners by using purchased chicken stock, but nothing has the energising, rejuvenating qualities of homemade chicken soup.

SERVES 6

Vietnamese beef noodle soup

185 g rice stick noodles

5—6 cups (1–1½ litres) beef stock

3 spring onions, sliced

2 thin slices fresh ginger, finely
shredded

150 g rump steak, thinly sliced

2 cups shredded mixed green
vegetables (bok choy, wombok,
silverbeet)

¾ cup fresh bean sprouts,
rinsed and drained

fish sauce

12 fresh mint, Vietnamese mint
or basil leaves

2—3 teaspoons chopped roasted
peanuts (optional)

Soften the noodles in boiling water for about 3 minutes, and drain.

Bring stock to the boil and add ginger and spring onions. Simmer
for 2–3 minutes.

Add meat, greens and bean sprouts and simmer for 1–2 minutes.

Season to taste with fish sauce, and stir in herbs.

Serve into large bowls, adding peanuts (if using).

SERVES 2

Corn chowder with crunchy tortilla chips

3 medium potatoes, peeled and
  diced

salt

80 g smoked bacon, diced

1 small onion, finely chopped

½ celery stalk, finely chopped

2–3 sprigs fresh thyme or
  ⅓ teaspoon dried thyme

1½ tablespoons butter or light
  olive oil

2 cups milk

salt and freshly ground black
  pepper

200 g frozen corn kernels

2 tablespoons chopped parsley

2½ tablespoons gluten-free
  plain flour

½ cup cream (optional)

2 corn tortillas

extra oil, for frying

Boil the potatoes in well salted water to barely cover, for about 5 minutes.

In a non-stick pan sauté the bacon, onion, celery and thyme in the butter
or olive oil until onions are translucent.

Add to the potatoes and 2 cups of their cooking water, the milk, corn and
salt and pepper to taste.

Bring to the boil and simmer for 6–8 minutes until potatoes are falling apart
and corn is tender. >

Mix flour with 2–3 tablespoons cold water, and add ¾ cup hot stock. Mix well, and pour into the soup. Simmer for a few minutes, stirring to thicken.

Add the parsley and cream, if using, and check seasoning. Keep warm.

Cut tortillas into triangles and fry crisp in hot oil. Drain well.

Serve chowder into deep bowls and top with a few crisp tortilla chips or garnish with fresh thyme.

 1½ tablespoons fine cornmeal (polenta) can be cooked with the soup instead of thickening with flour.

SERVES 4–6

Asparagus with pine nuts & crisp crumb dressing

1 bunch slender fresh asparagus
  (about 12 spears)
2 tablespoons butter
1½ tablespoons fruity olive oil
1½ tablespoons pine nuts, chopped
½ cup gluten-free fresh breadcrumbs
salt and freshly ground black pepper
1 tablespoon grated parmesan cheese

Bring a frying pan of lightly salted water to the boil.

Add asparagus and simmer for 2–3 minutes, until barely tender. Drain and set aside.

Reheat the pan and add the butter and oil and when foamy, add pine nuts, breadcrumbs, salt and pepper and fry until the crumbs and nuts are golden, stirring frequently (about 1½ minutes).

Return the asparagus and warm in the dressing, then serve onto plates and add a sprinkle of parmesan. Serve at once.

SERVES 2–3

Japanese mushroom & buckwheat noodle soup

12 dried shiitake mushrooms, soaked in 2 cups
  boiling water for 20 minutes

1½ teaspoons Japanese dashi stock powder,
  or 2 teaspoons chicken stock powder

2–3 tablespoons gluten-free soy sauce or fish sauce

1 tablespoon Japanese sweet rice wine (mirin)
  (optional)

300 g buckwheat noodles (soba)

1–2 spring-onion greens, chopped

60 g baby spinach leaves

4 eggs (optional)

Strain the liquid from the soaked mushrooms through a fine sieve into a saucepan. Slice the mushrooms.

Add 1 litre water, stock powder and sliced mushrooms to the mushroom liquid and place over medium heat to bring to the boil. Reduce heat and simmer for about 15 minutes until mushrooms are tender.

Add soy or fish sauce and mirin (if using) and keep warm.

In another saucepan boil the noodles in salted water for about 6 minutes, until tender. Drain well and divide between four deep bowls. **>**

Add spinach and onion greens and pour on the hot stock.

In Japan, a raw egg is sometimes added to each soup bowl, earning the soup the name 'Gazing at the Moon'.

 Dried shiitake mushrooms give this soup more flavour than the fresh variety.

SERVES 4

Chilled summer soup

1 small continental cucumber or 2 Lebanese cucumbers

1 red salad onion, finely diced

¼ green capsicum, finely diced

2 large tomatoes, seeded and diced

¼ cup chopped mint

2–3 tablespoons chopped flat leaf parsley

½ cup tomato passata, purée or pasta sauce

1½ cups cold chicken or vegetable stock, or water

salt and freshly ground black pepper

2–3 tablespoons natural yoghurt (optional)

Cut unpeeled cucumbers in half lengthwise and scoop out seeds. Coarsely grate or finely dice and place in a glass bowl.

Add the remaining ingredients, except the yoghurt, and season to taste.

Add ¾ cup crushed ice or broken ice cubes or refrigerate for at least half an hour, to chill before serving. Garnish with a dollop of yoghurt (if using).

SERVES 4–6

Sweet things

Almond and hazelnut meal and desiccated coconut play a vital role in gluten-free baking, replacing flour in part or entirely in many recipes. The result is luxuriously dense and moist treats. Most popular cakes and tarts can be prepared with gluten-free alternatives, although you may prefer to avoid flour mixes which contain soy flour, as its distinctive flavour can intrude unless counterbalanced by strongly flavoured ingredients like chocolate, golden syrup or dates. Experiment by converting standard recipes to gluten free using your own flour blends and innovations. Mascarpone or tangy crème fraîche, Greek-style yoghurt, sour and whipped cream can replace commercial ice-cream, which may contain gluten based thickeners. Or try your hand at whipping up fresh custard-based ice-cream or fruit sorbets.

< Mango carpaccio with lime
mascarpone & passionfruit
(page 194)

Mango carpaccio with lime mascarpone & passionfruit

1 large mango, thinly sliced

3 tablespoons mascarpone

grated zest of 1 lime

2 tablespoons passionfruit pulp
  (with seeds)

icing sugar, for dusting (optional)

Arrange mango on two chilled plates. Fold lime zest into mascarpone and place a spoonful on each plate. Drizzle on passionfruit, and dust generously with icing sugar (if using).

Serve at once.

SERVES 2

Berry parfait

2 coconut macaroons or 1 single-serve
  meringue case
½–¾ cup fresh or frozen berries
½ cup whipped cream or mascarpone
2 scoops vanilla ice-cream (optional)
raspberry syrup (optional), to serve

Break up macaroons or meringues and layer in a parfait glass with the
berries, cream or mascarpone and ice-cream (if using). Finish with
raspberry syrup (if using).

SERVES 1

Sweet vermicelli pudding

125 g fine rice vermicelli

2 tablespoons clarified or unsalted butter

300 ml pouring cream

1½ cups full-cream milk

⅓ teaspoon cardamom seeds

3 tablespoons sugar

1–2 tablespoons sultanas

1–2 tablespoons chopped raw cashews
  or almonds, plus extra for garnish

1 teaspoon rosewater (optional)

Crumble the rice vermicelli and fry in the butter until lightly golden. Add remaining ingredients (except rosewater) and simmer until vermicelli is tender (3–5 minutes), adding extra milk if it becomes too thick.

Serve hot, warm or cold, sprinkled with rosewater (if using) and garnished with chopped nuts.

SERVES 4–6

Clafoutis

1 × 400-g can mixed berries or other fruit

2 eggs

2 tablespoons sugar

½ teaspoon vanilla extract

½ cup gluten-free self-raising flour

½ cup milk, plus 2 extra tablespoons

ice-cream or whipped cream, to serve

Preheat the oven to 180°C. $\left(360\,F°\right)$ – 400

Tip fruit into a strainer to drain thoroughly.

Brush a shallow oven dish with melted butter or vegetable oil.

With an electric mixer beat sugar, eggs and vanilla until light and creamy. Add flour and milk, adding some or all of the extra milk to make a smooth, slightly runny batter.

Spread berries into the prepared dish and cover with the batter.

Bake for about 30 minutes, until the top is golden-brown and a skewer inserted into the centre of the pudding comes out clean.

Serve hot with ice-cream or whipped cream.

SERVES 2

Apple-berry crumble tart

90 g butter, plus 1 teaspoon extra

⅓ cup soft brown sugar

100 g almond or hazelnut meal

2 eggs

2¼ cups gluten-free self-raising flour, preferably without soy

1 × 800-g can pie apples

4–5 tablespoons blackberry or raspberry jam

½–¾ cup mixed roasted cashews and macadamias, chopped

thick cream or ice-cream, to serve

Preheat the oven to 180°C. Thickly grease the base and sides of a 23-cm pie dish or springform cake tin with the extra butter.

In a food processor, cream butter and sugar until soft and smooth. Add nut meal, eggs and flour and pulse until mixed and crumbly and press two-thirds into the pan.

Mix apples and jam and spread over base. Mix chopped nuts with remaining dough and crumble over the fruit.

Bake for about 45 minutes until crumbs are golden-brown. Serve warm or at room temperature, with thick cream or ice-cream.

SERVES 8

Lemon & lime delicious

4 2 large eggs, separated
2 1 tablespoon softened butter
4 2 tablespoons gluten-free cornflour
2} grated zest and juice of 1 large lemon
grated zest and juice of 1 large lime
8-10 4–5 tablespoons fine white sugar
2½ 1¼ cups pouring cream *(600 - 700 mls)*
icing sugar, for dusting

— 360 F

Preheat the oven to 180°C. Grease a pie or quiche dish with butter. Using an electric mixer, beat egg whites to stiff peaks and tip into a bowl. Add butter, cornflour, egg yolks, sugar and the grated zest and juice to the mixer and beat well. Gradually add the cream, and then fold in the beaten whites.

Spread the mixture into the prepared dish and bake for about 30 minutes. When the top is golden-brown and the pudding set, remove from the oven and serve hot or cold, dusted with icing sugar.

To make individual serves, pour mixture into six small pots and reduce cooking time to 20–25 minutes or until the tops are golden.

SERVES 4

Sticky-date pecan cookies

1 cup gluten-free plain flour
¾ teaspoon gluten-free baking powder
½ cup chopped pitted dates
¼ cup chopped pecans
⅓ cup melted butter
1 egg, beaten
¼ cup soft brown sugar

Preheat the oven to 180°C.

Line a baking tray with baking paper.

Combine all of the ingredients, and roll into ten balls.

Press out on the baking tray and bake for about 18 minutes until brown and cooked.

Cool completely before storing in an airtight container.

MAKES 10

Popcorn pudding

5 cups plain popcorn
½ cup sultanas
½ cup sugar
2 cups milk

Preheat the oven to 180°C. Thickly butter a 4-cup oven dish.

Crush popcorn and pick over to remove any unpopped corn kernels. Combine popcorn, sultanas, sugar and milk and pour into the dish.

Bake for about 40 minutes until set and golden-brown on top.

Serve warm or cold.

SERVES 4

Banana caramel tarts

3–4 tablespoons shredded coconut

1 recipe shortcrust pastry (page 249)
   or coconut pastry (page 251)

1 x 380-g can Top 'n' Fill Caramel

6–7 bananas, sliced

whipped cream, to serve

Spread coconut on a microwave-safe plate covered with paper towel. Microwave for 1 minute at a time, until lightly golden. Remove and let cool (or carefully brown in a non-stick pan over medium heat).

Roll out pastry and line 7-cm or 10-cm tart shells. Bake and let cool. Spread caramel in the bottom of each tart shell and cover with sliced bananas. Generously mound or pipe whipped cream over and finish with toasted shredded coconut.

 For chocolate tarts, bring 100 ml thickened cream barely to the boil, then remove from heat. Whisk in 100 g dark chocolate until melted. Leave to cool, then whisk in an egg white, and if you like, a teaspoon of liqueur such as Tia Maria, brandy or rum. Spoon into tart shells and refrigerate until set (about 30 minutes).

MAKES ABOUT 12

Basic butter cake

125 g butter, at room temperature
½ cup fine white sugar
1½ teaspoons vanilla extract
2 large eggs, lightly beaten
¾ cup gluten-free self-raising flour
⅓ cup rice flour
⅓ cup gluten-free cornflour
1½ teaspoons gluten-free baking powder
3 tablespoons lukewarm milk

Preheat the oven to 180°C.

Brush the inside of a 23-cm spring form tin, or 20-cm square cake tin with melted butter and line the base with baking paper.

With an electric mixer cream butter and sugar until smooth and light. Add vanilla and an egg and beat well. Add the other egg and beat again.

Sift the flours and baking powder over the mixture and fold in, adding milk to make a smooth, moist batter. Spread in the tin and bake for about 35 minutes until the cake is firm and golden-brown. Test with a skewer in the middle of the cake, it should come out clean.

Let cool in the tin for a few minutes and then turn out onto a cake rack to cool.

This plain butter cake mix is very versatile.

To make cupcakes, three-quarters fill 18–24 cupcake papers with the batter and bake for about 12 minutes, or until firm and golden, then cool and ice.

To make lamingtons, bake the cake in a square tin and when cool cut into 12 squares. Spread 1½ cups desiccated coconut in a shallow tray, and in another shallow dish combine 2 cups icing sugar, ⅓ cup cocoa and ½ cup boiling water and mix well (adding extra water, as needed, to make a smooth chocolate dip). One by one dip the cake squares into the chocolate, coating each side, then roll in coconut and set aside to dry.

To make a tea cake, simply spread melted butter over the top of the cooked cake and sprinkle thickly with cinnamon sugar. For apple tea cake, coat thin slices of apple with cornflour and press into the top of the cake before baking.

To make an upside-down cake, brush the baking paper with melted butter and spread thickly with soft brown sugar, then cover evenly with thinly sliced pineapple or pear, before pouring in the cake batter. Once cooked, invert onto a plate to serve.

SERVES 8

Banana cake

2 very ripe ladies' finger bananas

2 eggs

½ cup sour cream

⅓ cup fine white sugar

1 teaspoon vanilla extract

⅓ cup extra light olive oil

1 teaspoon gluten-free baking powder

1 teaspoon ground cinnamon

2 cups gluten-free self-raising flour

CREAM CHEESE ICING

250 g softened cream cheese

50 g softened butter

1 teaspoon vanilla extract

500 g icing sugar

Preheat oven to 180°C. Grease a 20-cm round cake tin. In a food processor whip bananas, eggs, sour cream, sugar, vanilla and olive oil to a creamy liquid. Sift baking powder, cinnamon and flour into a bowl and fold in the banana mix.

Spread evenly in the prepared tin and bake for 35–45 minutes, until golden-brown on top, and a skewer inserted into the centre comes out clean. Let rest in the tin for a few minutes, then invert onto a cake cooling rack.

To make the icing, use a food processor or electric mixer to blend the cream cheese and butter. Add the vanilla extract, then mix in the sifted icing sugar until smooth. When the cake is completely cold, use a spatula to cover with the icing and serve.

SERVES 6

Marmalade polenta cake

2 cups milk

½ cup sugar

1 cup fine cornmeal (polenta)

1 whole egg

4 egg yolks

60 g unsalted butter, melted

grated zest of 2 lemons

3–4 tablespoons marmalade

whipped cream or mascarpone,
   to serve

Bring milk, 1½ cups water and sugar to the boil. Sprinkle in the polenta, stirring briskly and simmer until thick (25–30 minutes), stirring frequently.

Spread in a shallow bowl and set aside to cool.

Preheat the oven to 180°C. Grease a 23-cm cake tin and line the base with baking paper.

Beat egg and yolks, melted butter and lemon zest into the polenta, mixing well. Spread batter in the prepared tin and bake for about 35 minutes, until firm and dry.

Invert onto a plate and spread marmalade thickly over the top while still hot. Cool to room temperature and serve with whipped cream or mascarpone.

SERVES 8

Seriously chocolate cake

125 g butter

90 g sugar

2 eggs

¾ cup almond meal

1 teaspoon gluten-free baking powder

½ cup gluten-free self-raising flour

2 tablespoons cocoa

100 g dark cooking chocolate

icing sugar, for dusting

8 inches

Preheat oven to 180°C. Lightly grease a 20-cm cake tin or a square slice tin.

Cream butter and sugar together and add the eggs one at a time, beating well. Fold in almond meal, baking powder, flour and cocoa.

Break the chocolate into small squares and melt two thirds in a microwave oven, or in a bowl over simmering water. Stir into the batter. Chop the remaining chocolate and fold into the batter.

Spread mixture evenly in the prepared tin and bake for about 25 minutes until the edges look slightly dry and a skewer pressed into the centre comes out clean. Dust cake with icing sugar and cut into wedges to serve warm or cold.

 To make brownies, dust with cocoa or drinking chocolate powder and cut into squares when completely cold.

SERVES 8–12

Blueberry muffins

110 g butter

½ cup sugar

3 eggs

½ cup sour cream

1 cup gluten-free self-raising flour

¼ cup rice flour

1⅓ teaspoons gluten-free baking powder

1⅓ teaspoons ground ginger (optional)

¼ cup fine cornmeal (polenta)

1 cup fresh or frozen blueberries (if using frozen, thaw and drain well)

Preheat oven to 190°C. Lightly grease muffin tins, or line tins with cupcake papers.

Using an electric mixer beat sugar and butter until light and creamy. Add eggs one at a time, beating well after each. Beat in sour cream.

Sift flour, rice flour, baking powder and ginger into the bowl and add polenta. Stir thoroughly and fold in blueberries.

Divide mixture between muffin tins and bake for about 20 minutes, until golden-brown and cooked through when tested with a skewer.

Let cool for a few minutes in the tins before turning out.

MAKES 10

Date scones

2½ cups gluten-free self-raising flour
1½ teaspoons gluten-free baking powder
½ teaspoon salt
1 cup milk
½ cup sour cream
½ cup chopped pitted dates
extra milk, for glazing
butter or whipped cream, to serve

Preheat oven to 200°C.

Sift flour, baking powder and salt into a bowl. Add milk and cream to make a dough and fold in dates.

On a lightly floured board roll out dough to about 2-cm thick and cut into twelve rounds.

Line a baking tray with baking paper and transfer the scones, placing them fairly close together. Glaze with milk.

Bake for about 25 minutes, until golden-brown and cooked through.

Serve warm or cold, with butter or whipped cream.

MAKES 12

Coconut pikelets

½ cup desiccated coconut

⅓ cup rice flour

½ cup milk

1 egg

½ teaspoon gluten-free baking powder

2 teaspoons sugar

butter or oil, for frying

In a bowl combine all of the ingredients (except the butter or oil) and let sit for 10 minutes.

Heat a hot plate, electric frying pan or large non-stick pan to medium with the butter or oil, and fry tablespoons of the mixture for about 40 seconds on the first side, and about 30 seconds on the other side, until golden-brown and puffy.

Serve with honey or maple syrup and butter, or puréed berries with ice-cream, mascarpone or whipped cream.

MAKES 9–10

Coconut macaroons

2 large egg whites

1 cup desiccated coconut

2 tablespoons rice flour

⅔ cup caster sugar

1–2 teaspoons grated lemon zest (optional)

Preheat oven to 180°C.

Line a biscuit tin or baking tray with baking paper.

Beat egg whites to stiff peaks and fold in coconut, flour, sugar and zest (if using), and mix well.

Form little mounds of the batter on the tray and bake for about 20 minutes, until lightly golden-brown.

Cool on a rack before storing.

To make almond macaroons, replace coconut with almond meal and use only 1 tablespoon rice flour. Form into balls with wet hands and roll in flaked almonds before baking.

MAKES 12

Golden syrup biscuits

1 cup gluten-free plain flour
¾ teaspoon gluten-free baking powder
¼ cup butter
¼ cup golden syrup

Preheat oven to 180°C.

Line a small baking tray with baking paper.

Sift flour and baking powder into a bowl.

In a small heatproof dish melt butter and syrup together in the microwave on high for 1 minute. Stir into flour and roll into twelve balls.

Place on the paper allowing space between them, and flatten slightly with a fork dipped in flour.

Bake for 15 minutes, let cool and store in an airtight container.

MAKES 12

Quick no-bake coconut lemon slice

1 cup gluten-free biscuit crumbs

60 g melted butter

1½ cups desiccated coconut

¾ cup lemon curd

Combine biscuit crumbs and melted butter, mix well and press into a 14-cm square cake tin lined with baking paper.

Mix 1¼ cups coconut with the lemon curd and spread over the base.

Cover the slice with remaining coconut, pressing on lightly.

Cover with plastic wrap and chill for at least 1 hour before cutting into 4-cm squares to serve.

MAKES 18

Fruit & nut chocolate crunch bars

3 cups cornflakes

⅔ cup finely chopped dried fruit (sultanas,
    raisins, dates, apple, etc.)

2–3 tablespoons finely chopped mixed nuts

⅓ cup icing sugar

½ cup melted butter

150 g dark cooking chocolate

Crush cornflakes and mix with fruit, nuts, icing sugar and melted butter, stirring evenly.

Spread on a piece of baking paper or onto edible rice paper.

Melt chocolate over simmering water, or carefully in a microwave oven, and spread or drizzle evenly over the slice.

Cut into bars and chill to set.

Separate the bars when firm, and store in a covered container in the refrigerator.

MAKES 18

Egg custard

2 tablespoons arrowroot or cornflour
1 tablespoon gluten-free plain flour
2–3 tablespoons fine white sugar
1–1¾ cups milk
1½ teaspoons vanilla extract
2 egg yolks (optional)

Combine arrowroot or cornflour, plain flour, sugar and ¾ cup milk in a saucepan and stir over medium-high heat using a wooden spoon. When it comes to the boil reduce heat to medium-low and continue to cook, stirring all the time, until it thickens. Remove from the heat and stir in half the remaining milk and the vanilla. Use a balloon whisk to incorporate, and then return to the heat and simmer until it thickens. (For a thinner custard, add the remaining milk.)

Remove from the heat and whisk in egg yolks, and then cook for 1–2 minutes more, again stirring all the time.

 Add melted chocolate or cocoa to make chocolate custard. If you're an ice-cream addict, churn and freeze your own using this basic egg custard.

MAKES 2 CUPS

Quick peach crumble

1 × 410-g can sliced peaches

60 g butter

¼ cup soft brown sugar

⅓ cup gluten-free self-raising flour

¾ cup rice porridge, desiccated coconut
   or rice crumbs

whipped cream, to serve

Preheat oven to 190°C.

Drain peaches thoroughly, and spread in a small oven dish.

Place butter, sugar, flour and rice porridge, crumbs or coconut in a food processor and chop to crumbs.

Spread evenly over the peaches and bake for about 20 minutes until the top is golden-brown. Serve with whipped cream.

SERVES 4

Bread, dough & pastry

Gluten-free bread is widely stocked these days, fresh in specialist bakeries and health food stores, fresh or frozen at the supermarket. There are also reliable brands of bread mix which require minimal effort and give good results. But these easy-bake recipes offer interesting variety without much effort in the kitchen.

As gluten provides elasticity to flour, gluten-free flour reacts differently and requires additives to provide the rise and softness we like in our bread and pizza bases. Gluten-free flour is now sold in most supermarkets. It contains a combination of different flours, which may include rice, potato, tapioca, corn (maize) and soy. Self-raising flour has bicarbonate of soda and cream of tartare, or baking powder added as a rising agent.

< White bread & rolls (page 233)

Some good examples of homemade gluten-free flours are provided opposite. Or you may like to test your own formula using the standard gluten-free flours — maize cornflour, rice flour, tapioca starch and soy flour. There are also a number of other gluten-free starches and flours which can be added for extra flavour or their thickening qualities. These are arrowroot and potato starch, brown rice, buckwheat, chestnut, chickpea and glutinous rice flours. Fine cornmeal polenta adds a delicious texture to cakes, bread and muffins.

Gluten is what gives dough its elasticity and soft texture. Some manufacturers of organic food produce ready-to-use gluten substitute mixes which when added to gluten-free flour equate with the qualities of normal wheat flour when it comes to rising, texture and softness. The vegetable gums xanthan and guar, and glutinous (sticky) rice flour can all contribute to compensating for the absence of gluten in baking flour. Gluten-free bread dough is generally softer, requiring loaf tins and muffin pans for cooking. When transposing from a standard non-gluten-free recipe, increase the amount of raising agent used.

Cornbread is a welcome addition to a limited bread repertoire, as are store-bought corn tortillas, and gluten-free flatbread which can be made into wraps and several varieties of popular Indian bread.

GLUTEN-FREE PLAIN FLOUR 1

500 g rice flour

120 g potato flour

90 g tapioca flour

3 teaspoons xanthan or guar gum (as a gluten substitute)

GLUTEN-FREE PLAIN FLOUR 2

400 g rice flour

100 g soy flour

120 g potato flour

90 g tapioca flour

3 teaspoons xanthan or guar gum (as a gluten substitute)

SELF-RAISING FLOUR

Add 1½ teaspoons bicarbonate of soda and 1 teaspoon cream of tartar to either of the above recipes.

Making breadcrumbs is a sensible way to use up the ends of a loaf of gluten-free bread. Use them for crumbing and coating to give a crunchy topping to vegetables and bakes, and in stuffing and fillings.

For soft fresh crumbs, trim hard crusts from gluten-free bread and break into small cubes. Place in a food processor or blender and chop to coarse crumbs. Store in a plastic container in the freezer so they are ready whenever you need them. For dried crumbs, dry the bread slices in a low oven for several hours, or dehydrate in the microwave (taking care the bread does not burn or catch fire). When cool, crush with a rolling pin or chop in a blender or food processor and store in an airtight container.

White bread & rolls

3 cups gluten-free plain flour

1½ teaspoons salt

2 teaspoons fine white sugar

1½ cups milk

14 g dried yeast

Grease a 20-cm × 14-cm loaf tin or a 12-hole muffin pan.

Sift flour, salt and sugar into a bowl and make a well in the centre.

Mix 1 cup hot water with the milk and test with a finger, it should be lukewarm, if too warm set aside for a few minutes to cool. Mix in the yeast and pour over the flour, mixing in well.

Spread batter in the loaf tin or muffin pans and let sit in a warm part of the kitchen to rise for about 20 minutes for rolls, 30–35 minutes for the bread loaf.

Preheat the oven to 180°C and bake the rolls for about 20 minutes or the loaf for 45 minutes to 1 hour, until cooked through and lightly browned on top.

Spraying the top of the loaf with olive oil several times during cooking may encourage browning. >

When cooked, let loaf cool in the tin for 6–7 minutes, rolls for 1–2 minutes before turning out onto a rack.

 This is a simple white milk bread with a satisfying texture. As it contains none of the standard additives to keep it moist and fresh, take what is needed for the day, then slice and pack the remainder into a plastic container or zip-lock bags to keep in the freezer. When using dried yeast, check the use-by date – it can lose its effectiveness if kept too long.

MAKES 1 LOAF OR 12 ROLLS

Pumpkin & pepita bread

500 g packet gluten-free bread mix

1 cup cooked pumpkin, smoothly mashed
   (about 250 g raw pumpkin)

2–3 tablespoons pepitas

1–2 tablespoons sunflower seeds

2 tablespoons chopped parsley or
   2½ teaspoons chopped rosemary

1 teaspoon dried oregano or rosemary

Preheat the oven to 190°C. Tip bread mix into a bowl and make a well in the centre. In another bowl mix the required liquid for the bread mix with the pumpkin, beating well. Pour into the flour and mix in, adding half the pepitas, sunflower seeds and all of the chopped herbs.

Grease a loaf tin and sprinkle with most of the remaining pepitas and sunflower seeds. Transfer bread batter to the prepared tin and scatter on remaining seeds.

Let rise for the required time, then bake for about 35 minutes. Test with a skewer after 30 minutes. If the skewer comes out clean and dry the bread is ready. Let sit in the tin for 2–3 minutes, then turn onto a rack to cool.

MAKES 1 LOAF

Sun-dried tomato & herb muffins

1½ cups gluten-free self-raising flour

1 teaspoon gluten-free baking powder

½ teaspoon salt

½ teaspoon dried oregano or 1½ tablespoons
   finely grated parmesan cheese

2 tablespoons chopped fresh basil or flat leaf parsley

1½ tablespoons finely chopped sun-dried tomatoes

80 g softened butter

2 eggs

¾ cup milk

Preheat the oven to 190°C. Spray a muffin tin with olive oil.

Sift the flour, baking powder and salt into a bowl. Add dried herbs
or parmesan, fresh herbs and tomatoes and mix well.

Beat butter and eggs together until creamy, and whisk in milk.

Stir into the flour mixture and divide evenly between the muffin tins.

Bake for 15–18 minutes until golden on the surface. Test with a skewer
in the centre of a muffin. It should come out clean. Serve warm or cold.

MAKES 8 LARGE MUFFINS

Cornbread

¾ cup fine cornmeal (polenta)

¾ cup gluten-free self-raising flour

¾ teaspoon salt

1 teaspoon gluten-free baking powder

2 teaspoons sugar

3 eggs

100 g melted butter

⅓ cup milk or ½ cup creamed corn

2 tablespoons chopped parsley (optional)

Preheat the oven to 180°C. Grease a loaf tin or muffin pan and set aside.

Combine cornmeal, flour, salt and baking powder in a bowl. In another bowl beat eggs with sugar, melted butter and milk or corn. Add to the dry ingredients and mix in well, stirring in the herbs (if using).

Spread batter in the prepared loaf or muffin tin and bake for about 20 minutes until golden-brown and firm. Test by inserting a skewer into the centre of the bread, it should come out clean.

Let sit in the tin for 3–4 minutes, and then turn out on a cake rack to cool. >

To make spicy Mexican cornbread, add 1½ teaspoons paprika and 1–2 teaspoons finely chopped red chilli. Parsley can be replaced with coriander.

MAKES 1 LOAF OR 8 SMALL CAKES

Flatbread & wraps

½ cup gluten-free cornflour

1 cup gluten-free plain flour

½ cup gluten substitute (gluten-free gluten)

1 teaspoon salt

½ teaspoon gluten-free baking powder

2½ tablespoons light olive oil

Sift flours, gluten substitute, salt and baking powder into a bowl and make a well in the centre. Add the oil and ¾ cup lukewarm water and mix to a soft, but not sticky dough.

Remove from the bowl and knead on a lightly floured surface for 2–3 minutes. Roll into a sausage shape.

For chapatis and rotis cut into eight pieces and roll or press out into thin rounds.

For pita and wraps cut into six pieces. Roll or press pita into rounds about 8 mm thick and for wraps roll out as thin as possible.

Heat a heavy-based non-stick pan over medium heat. Cook one or two pieces at a time, without oil, until the surface becomes lightly browned and bubbly. >

Encourage the bread to puff by gently pressing in the centre with a balled-up paper towel. Turn and cook the other side.

Layer cooked bread with paper towels and wrap in foil to keep warm and pliable while the remainder are cooked.

 To make puffy, crisp puris (fried chapatis), roll dough into 8–10 rounds and fry in shallow oil until golden and puffy. Drain well before serving. This useful recipe is very versatile. Use it to make pita style flat bread, soft wraps, Indian chapatis and rotis, puris and with a bit of extra manipulation (see next recipe) you can also have flaky parathas. Substitute gluten-free flatbread for flour tortillas in any Mexican recipe.

MAKES 6–8

Flaky Indian bread (parathas)

1 recipe flatbread (page 241)
2–3 tablespoons oil, or melted ghee or butter
1 cup oil (optional), for frying

Roll the dough into a sausage shape and cut into 5–6 pieces.

Brush a worktop with oil and roll out the dough until very thin. Brush with oil or melted ghee, pleat into a strip, then twist the strip into a coil.

Brush with more oil or ghee and roll out reasonably thin.

Heat a hotplate and cook the bread to golden-brown, turning once or twice. Brush with ghee and keep warm while the remaining parathas are cooked. Alternatively, heat oil in a large pan and fry parathas, turning once, until crisp and golden.

Serve hot.

MAKES 5–6

Spicy chickpea flour bread

¾ cup besan (chickpea flour)
1¼ cups gluten-free plain flour
⅓ teaspoon ground turmeric
1 teaspoon garam masala
1 teaspoon salt + garlic (powder)
2 tablespoons finely chopped fresh coriander
2 tablespoons finely chopped onion
a little chopped fresh red chilli (optional)
oil, for frying (optional)

Sift flours, salt and spices together into a bowl. Add coriander, onion and chilli (if using), and enough water to make a firm but workable dough.

Wrap in plastic and leave for 20 minutes, then roll into a sausage shape and divide into eight pieces.

On a lightly floured board roll each piece out into a thin round.

Heat a hotplate and cook the bread, several pieces at a time, until the underside is flecked with brown. Turn and cook the other side.

Wrap cooked flatbread in a cloth until ready to serve. >

Alternately, heat about 4 cm oil in a pan and fry the bread until puffy and golden, about 45 seconds on each side.

 You can also use this dough as a spicy pastry for tartlets. Line small, lightly oiled tart tins, prick the base and bake at 200°C for about 12 minutes, until dry and golden-brown. Add a spicy filling and serve with yoghurt and chutney.

MAKES 8

Thin-crust pizza base

2 × 7-g sachets dried yeast

2 teaspoons fine white sugar

2 cups gluten-free plain flour

1½ tablespoons gluten substitute
   (gluten-free gluten) (optional)

¾ teaspoon salt

1 tablespoon olive oil

In a small bowl mix the yeast and sugar with ¼ cup lukewarm water and whisk with a fork until it begins to bubble. Let sit for 10 minutes, whisking occasionally, until it becomes slightly thicker and creamy.

Combine flour, gluten substitute (if using) and salt in a mixing bowl and make a well in the centre. Add the yeast mixture and 1 cup lukewarm water and quickly work to a soft dough adding water as needed to make a very soft, but not quite sticky dough. Cover the bowl and let sit for 30 minutes in a warm part of the kitchen. The dough will rise slightly.

Turn out onto a floured surface and knead lightly. Cut dough in half and roll each out into a ball.

To par-cook the pizza base for later use, lightly grease 2-cm × 23-cm pizza tray or 1 large tray. >

With oiled fingers press the dough into a thin round on the tray and prick with a fork. Let sit while oven heats to 220°C.

Brush pizza base with olive oil and bake for 12–15 minutes. The pizza base will be dry and firm and very lightly golden on the edges.

Allow to cool completely before wrapping in plastic wrap and storing in the refrigerator for 1–2 days, or in the freezer.

(To use prebaked pizza base, thaw frozen base, spread lightly with olive oil and desired toppings and bake at 250°C for 10–15 minutes.)

 For garlic pizza bread, brush pizza base with oil mixed with crushed garlic, add flake salt, thyme or rosemary leaves and a fine covering of grated melting cheese and bake for about 15 minutes to golden-brown.

MAKES TWO 23-CM PIZZA BASES OR 1 FAMILY-SIZE PIZZA BASE

13 April — it works!

Shortcrust pastry

1¼ cups gluten-free plain flour
½ teaspoon salt
100 g butter, cut into small cubes
1 large egg

Sift flour into a food processor and add salt and the butter cubes and process until grainy. Add the egg and work in using the pulse control. If it seems dry add 1–3 teaspoons water, but do not overwork.

Tip onto a worktop and bring together into a smooth ball, kneading lightly but without handling it too much.

Roll out between two sheets of baking paper lightly dusted with flour and transfer to a tart or pie dish. Trim edges and prick base with a fork. Refrigerate for 20–30 minutes.

Preheat oven to 180°C.

Bake pastry shell for about 20 minutes, until lightly golden. Increase heat to 240°C and brown for about 5 minutes. Switch off the oven and let the pastry remain inside for about 10 minutes to dry out, or add filling and bake for up to 40 minutes, as required. ➤

When making quiches and savoury tarts and pies you can add any of the following: 2 tablespoons finely grated parmesan cheese, 2–3 tablespoons finely chopped fresh herbs, 1½ teaspoons crumbled dried oregano or a mix of oregano and thyme.

To make sweet shortcrust pastry, add 1½ tablespoons icing sugar to the shortcrust pastry recipe and proceed in the same way, using only 2 teaspoons cold water.

To make chocolate pastry, add 2 tablespoons cocoa to the sweet pastry mix, and 1–2 teaspoons cold water.

For a covered deep dish pie, make double the quantity of pastry.

MAKES 23-CM TART SHELL OR QUICHE BASE

Coconut pastry

2 egg whites

½ cup icing sugar

2 tablespoons gluten-free cornflour
or arrowroot

1¾ cups desiccated coconut

Whisk egg whites to fluffy and stir in icing sugar, cornflour or arrowroot and coconut. Moisten with very little water or extra egg white if dry.

With wet fingers press pastry into tart tins in a thin, even layer and chill for 10 minutes.

Preheat the oven to 180°C and bake for about 10 minutes, until golden.

 Use this crunchy-chewy pastry for rich chocolate, caramel, sweet cheese and banana cream fillings.

MAKES 23-CM TART SHELL OR 10–12 SMALL TARTS

Conversions

OVEN TEMPERATURES

Celsius	Fahrenheit
160 °C	320°F
170 °C	340°F
180 °C	360°F
190 °C	375°F
200 °C	390°F
220 °C	430°F
240 °C	465°F

WEIGHTS

Grams	Ounces
15 g	½ oz
25 g	1 oz
50 g	2 oz
80 g	3 oz
100 g	3½ oz
150 g	5 oz
175 g	6 oz
250 g	9 oz
375 g	13 oz
500 g	16 oz (1 lb)
750 g	1 lb 5 oz
1 kg	2 lb

LIQUIDS

Cups/spoons	Millilitres	Fluid ounces
1 teaspoon	5 ml	⅕ fl oz
1 tablespoon	20 ml	¾ fl oz
¼ cup	60 ml	2 fl oz
⅓ cup	80 ml	2¾ fl oz
½ cup	125 ml	4½ fl oz
1 cup	250 ml	8 fl oz
	400 ml	13½ fl oz
	600 ml	20 fl oz (1 pint)

SIZES

Centimetres	Inches
1 cm	⅖ in
3 cm	1⅕ in
5 cm	2 in
7 cm	2⅘ in
12 cm	5 in
18 cm	7 in
20 cm	8 in
23 cm	9 in

Index

PENGUIN BOOKS

Published by the Penguin Group
Penguin Group (Australia)
250 Camberwell Road, Camberwell, Victoria 3124, Australia
(a division of Pearson Australia Group Pty Ltd)
Penguin Group (USA) Inc.
375 Hudson Street, New York, New York 10014, USA
Penguin Group (Canada)
90 Eglinton Avenue East, Suite 700, Toronto, Canada ON M4P 2Y3
(a division of Pearson Penguin Canada Inc.)
Penguin Books Ltd
80 Strand, London WC2R 0RL, England
Penguin Ireland
25 St Stephen's Green, Dublin 2, Ireland
(a division of Penguin Books Ltd)
Penguin Books India Pvt Ltd
11 Community Centre, Panchsheel Park, New Delhi – 110 017, India
Penguin Group (NZ)
67 Apollo Drive, Rosedale, North Shore 0632, New Zealand
(a division of Pearson New Zealand Ltd)
Penguin Books (South Africa) (Pty) Ltd
24 Sturdee Avenue, Rosebank, Johannesburg 2196, South Africa

Penguin Books Ltd, Registered Offices: 80 Strand, London, WC2R 0RL, England

First published by Penguin Group (Australia) 2009

10 9 8 7 6 5 4 3 2 1

Many thanks go to Market Imports in Armadale who provided a selection of their beautiful props.

Cover and text design by Marley Flory © Penguin Group (Australia)
Photographs by Julie Renouf
Food styling by Lee Blaylock
Typeset by Post Pre-Press Group, Brisbane, Queensland
Scanning and separations by Splitting Image P/L, Clayton, Victoria
Printed and bound in China by Everbest Printing Co. Ltd

National Library of Australia
Cataloguing-in-Publication data:

    Passmore, Jacki
    Gluten Free Bible
    ISBN 978 0 14 3011514 (pbk.)
    Includes index
    1. Gluten-free diet-recipes

    641.56318

penguin.com.au